Norman Hapgood

Literary Statesmen and others

Essays on Men seen from a Distance

Norman Hapgood

Literary Statesmen and others
Essays on Men seen from a Distance

ISBN/EAN: 9783337186234

Printed in Europe, USA, Canada, Australia, Japan

Cover: Foto ©ninafisch / pixelio.de

More available books at **www.hansebooks.com**

LITERARY STATESMEN

AND OTHERS

Literary Statesmen

And Others

Essays on Men seen from a Distance

BY

NORMAN HAPGOOD

HERBERT S. STONE & CO.

CHICAGO & NEW YORK

M DCCC XCVII

CONTENTS

LORD ROSEBERY

LITERARY STATESMEN AND OTHERS

I

LORD ROSEBERY

LORD ROSEBERY, who has naturally been studied mainly as a statesman, appears, in the little he has written with an eye to literary form, as an artist of marked qualities, of talents which are high, although they do not combine into genius. A reader of the "Life of Pitt," or of various addresses, or even of some of the political speeches, must feel that the most significant element of the style is charm, composed largely of humor which is gay but not frivolous, of seriousness which is usually far from solemn, and of a taste which, never obtrusive, gives the suggestion of culture to every phrase.

Of these elements the humor is the most individual, and so near akin to other qualities that it will bear dwelling on. It is never caustic, but friendly and pervasive, often even merry, altogether inspired by temperament. "The son of the respected family physician, who had prescribed colchicum to the elder and port to the younger Pitt, Addington carried into politics the indefinable air of a village apothecary inspecting the tongue of the State." These words are spontaneous, real fun, expressing the overflow of a personality, not at all the studied wit of a clever man, and therefore not at all consistent with the popular notion that Lord Rosebery used to sit in his office in the House of Lords, in a chair tipped back, looking into vacancy for happy phrases. If he were seen in that occupation the enjoyment would be greater and the effort less than a description of the attitude would suggest. "A strategist of unalloyed incompetency and unvaried failure," although less expansive than the other quotation, has the true ring of fun in it.

"'You should forget party,' said the Duke of Argyll. . . . The Duke of Argyll cannot forget his party, because his party is himself. Whatever may be your wishes, however noble may be your aspirations, when you have a party in that compact and singular, I might almost say that portable, form, it is one of which you cannot divest yourself, and it is one of which I think the Duke, on reflection, would be unwilling to divest himself."

In the same speech he said: —

"Now, if all hope of union has not fled before this, it is due, in my opinion, mainly to the patience of our leaders, who, when they have been buffeted on one cheek, have meekly offered the other. But I am bound to say this, that the time may come when we shall come to an end both of our patience and of our cheeks."

It is only fair, since his treatment of humor is to be used as an indication of Lord Rosebery's general character, to put in contrast to these expressions of easy and genial amusement an example of his crudities, which are extremely rare, and sometimes comical, in spite of their artificiality. "By a strange accident, he became the leader of the nobility; but they supported him on their necks, for his foot was there."

That humor may fairly be called a central point of Lord Rosebery's character is indicated by the kinship between that quality and the others in which he is attractive. Next to brilliancy of isolated perceptions, taste is the most essential element of humor, and Lord Rosebery's seldom errs. In his frequent references to art and literature there is no suggestion of pedantry. In his most earnest passages there is seldom declamation. Padding of all kinds, repetitions, adjectives employed to give sound, all the ordinary faults, are absent. There is no great subtlety, no pretentious paradox, no lack of calm and sure literary judgment. Dulness, above all, is a thing the writer abhors, even more, if possible, than grossness. In the "Life of Pitt," perhaps, of all the excellences the most conspicuous is a speed of style resulting altogether from this avoidance of clogging or distracting errors, a speed which suggests not haste but clearness of thought and the restraint of culture, and is as noticeable in the comment as in the pure narrative. The felicity of phrase, although varying in degree, is always prominent enough to add to the faultlessness of the style a constant positive charm. "But these are like the wars of Marlborough and Turenne, — splendid achievements, which light up the epoch, without exercising a permanent influence on the world; to us, at any rate, the sheet-lightning of history." No single phrase could be found to give the quality of Lord Rosebery's half-humorous imagination better than this metaphor. His characterizations of persons, also, even when they are serious, have a dash allied to wit. "He charmed equally the affections of Carlyle and Fitzpatrick, the meteoric mind of Burke, the pedantic vanity of Parr, the austere virtue of Horner, and the hedgehog soul of Rogers." Any number of passages to show this pervading, graceful, friendly irony might be found.

> "The uneasy whisper circulated, and the joints of the lords became as water. The peers, who yearned for lieutenancies or regiments, for stars or strawberry leaves; the prelates, who sought a larger sphere of usefulness; the minions of the bed-chamber and the janissaries of the closet; all, temporal or spiritual, whose convictions were unequal to their appetite, rallied to the royal nod."

Certainly these genial touches do not lack picturesqueness. They must please a cultivated man with a combination of grace and vividness which comes just to the edge of imagination, near enough to borrow some of its attractiveness. It might be said, perhaps, that Lord Rosebery appreciates imagination, and has some of it, but is unable to give it to his style. A passage coming as near to it as any is this: —

> "It was in Holland that his first complication arose. On that familiar board all the great powers of Europe were moving their pawns, — the fitful philanthropist, Joseph the Second, who had opened the games with his usual disastrous energy; the old

fox at Berlin; the French monarchy, still bitten with the suicidal mania of fermenting republics against Great Britain; and the crafty voluptuary of St. Petersburg."

Lord Rosebery comes within sight both of literary and political imagination, and is kept from reaching them by traits which are at once his powers and his limitations. Taste and appreciation can take him no farther than this. Clearness and measure put him down at a point from which he should be carried on by emotion and will, if he were to add to the intelligence which he has the power which he lacks. Some passages reach nobility, none reaches grandeur; many are persuasive, none is compelling. What is lacking is as necessary to a philosopher or a poet as it is to a man of action. It is easiest, perhaps, to see it as a moral weakness, although it is of equal importance from the æsthetic and the practical sides. It is a want of unity, of strong single feeling, of purpose. His perceptions, like his efforts, are unsustained and unrelated, lacking in concentration and therefore in force. There is honesty, frankness, generosity; there are convictions; but there is no single unifying conviction or conception, no faith, or passion, or need of accomplishment. So it is that the more serious the subject, the farther removed from the spectacular intellectual world, the nearer to a reality demanding action, the less adequate is Lord Rosebery in speaking or writing. As long as the tone is light, the unrelated brilliant flashes, the frequent pleasant places, seem sufficient; but when the moral sense is aroused, when force and massing power are needed, impressiveness is called for. From the last citation, which was a success, it is but a step to others just as well written, but none the less, on account of their subjects, failures. Fairness, truth, and clearness, are pleasing always, but color and warmth, the inspiration of a character, are needed to make some ideas live. The political aspect of this very general truth has been stated, somewhat unsympathetically, by Lord Rosebery himself:

"Few supreme parliamentary speeches have perhaps ever been delivered by orators who have been unable to convince themselves, not absolutely that they are in the right, but that their opponents are absolutely in the wrong, and the most abandoned of scoundrels to boot, for holding a contrary opinion. No less a force, no feebler flame than this, will sway or incense the mixed temperaments of mankind."

But that is only the more paltry side of the popular demand for a strong and lasting faith, and for devotion to its requirements. Again Lord Rosebery speaks for himself: "Fox could, indeed, lay down principles for all time; but the moment the game was afoot, they ceased to govern his conduct." With this may be put his assertion that "the English love a statesman whom they can understand, or at least think they can understand." What they sympathetically comprehend is rather earnestness and power than grace and neutral justice. After a paragraph in which he sums up the most important influences on Pitt's childhood, Lord Rosebery remarks, "All this does not amount to much;" and he repeats identically the same phrase after talking of Pitt's literary tastes. It is not true; it is an expression of self-consciousness, and a small thing could hardly illustrate more clearly the weakness of mere refinement, judged even by literary standards.

To reconcile the assertion that Lord Rosebery is serious with the assertion that his greatest failure is moral, would be to draw a line with exactness about his character. Not only is he gifted, refined, and elegant, but he has qualities more distinctly moral, such as courage and openness; but these moral elements are what might be called negative. His virtues are inactive, and therefore depressing to most men. Like the famous creation of Buridan, he sees so clearly the reasonableness of opposite courses that he stands motionless. It is easy to see a relation between the enthusiasm, the spirit, the self abandonment that are necessary to a moving style and the power of final decision in action; and the literary as well as the practical defect is conspicuous in Lord Rosebery. Nothing could make him commit a wrong. Not even popularity, which he likes, could lead him to speak a disingenuous word, or do the smallest act in which he did not believe. His speech at Edinburgh, after his resignation from the leadership, was strong in calm veracity and generosity. It is easy to grow enthusiastic in thinking of such virtues, and it is with sadness that one who is won as much by his integrity as by his culture sees how little these things avail to give greatness or importance when the possessor lacks moral authority.

Certainly mere grace could hardly be more perfect than it is in the Edinburgh speech. What could have a better tone than the reference to the old leader who had just helped to show the world his *protégé's* failure?

"Perhaps Mr. Gladstone has been the indirect cause, or the latest indirect cause, of the action that I have thought right to take, and to which you have alluded. But let none think that for that reason I have regretted his intervention in the Armenian question. It is now seventeen years ago since Mr. Gladstone came to Midlothian. I remember then making a speech in which I said that we welcomed the sight of a great statesman, full of years and full of honors, coming down at his advanced period of life to fight one supreme battle on behalf of liberty in Europe. Little did I think then that seventeen years later I should see a still nobler sight — a statesman — the same statesman — fuller still of years, and, if possible, still fuller of honors, coming out and leaving a well-earned retirement, which the whole nation watches with tenderness and solicitude, to fight another battle, but I hope not the last, on behalf of the principles in which his life has been spent."

The cartoons show us Lord Rosebery quietly reading in his study, while the Armenians perish. Under the brutal exaggeration is the truth that in no emergency does he lose his literary interest, that it is his distinction and his limitation to be always in the artistic attitude. In this same speech, in one of its most earnest and significant passages, he can stop to give his hearers a piece of literary counsel: —

"Cromwell interfered, it is true, on behalf of people oppressed much as these Armenians are. He wrote, or rather he signed, some letters on that subject, which were written by John Milton and signed by Oliver Cromwell, — an august conjunction, — which in their agony and vehemence of pathos still thrill our hearts across the generations that separate us. And, gentlemen, if this Eastern question has no other result than this to you, I hope it will make you betake yourselves to those sublime despatches."

In prose, in short, Lord Rosebery is impeccable. Seldom has he tried to leap beyond this boundary; but the one time I know of when he did endeavor to glorify his feeling and his language, to put into his words the color of poetry, he failed with pitiable completeness. When he tried to put explicitly the deeper feelings, which to be convincingly expressed must be spoken in quite a different tone, he produced something of which it is hardly too much to say that, honest in feeling as it is, it is in the result mere declamation.

"In this place, and in this day, it all seems present to us, — the house of anguish, the thronged churchyard, the weeping neighbors. We feel ourselves part of the mourning crowd; we hear their volleys and their muffled drums; we bow our heads as the coffin passes, and acknowledge with tears the inevitable doom. Pass, heavy hearse, with thy weary ſreight of shattered hopes and exhausted frame; pass with thy simple pomp of fatherless bairns, and sad, moralizing friends; pass with the sting of death to the victory of the grave; pass with the perishable, and leave us the eternal."

There is no passion in all this, there is only calm observation, trying to speak a language more affecting than its own. It is not the real Rosebery at all.

Or, rather, it is not the Rosebery his fairest admirers spontaneously think of. Their Rosebery comes back to them when, in the same speech, he calls puff and advertisement "intellectual cosmetics," frail and fugitive, rarely surviving their subject. This is the laughing Lord Rosebery, easy, happy in wit and shrewd perceptions, pleasing gifts, and attractive personality; the man who in his boyhood is said to have planned out his future as a brilliant show, calmly deciding to be Prime Minister and to win the Derby; the statesman whose whole career has been an illustration of the futility in large action of a mind which in sport is so charming. What more natural than that his shrewdness and elegance should even trouble the average Englishman, should certainly be no compensation, since the average Englishman is so much that Lord Rosebery is not? The average Englishman is a man of action, of unconscious poetry in sentiment but of little artistic feeling, positive, prejudiced, and efficient. Lord Rosebery's is in an extreme degree the critical temperament, and three doubters, as some Frenchman put it, do not equal one believer. The detached, sceptical, literary temperament has, as a rule, been distrusted by the masses; and England as a whole, although it has followed men who enjoyed artistic pursuits as side issues, has never followed anybody in whom the artistic qualities were more prominent than the moral and active ones. The people do not admire a man who hates to move until he is convinced on logical grounds, any more than they admire in their intellectual world a thinker who has only rationality. Doubtless men of Lord Rosebery's kind, "corrective sceptics," help to increase culture; but as individuals they are seldom important in life or letters. "A constitutional statesman," says Bagehot, "is in general a man of common ideas and uncommon abilities." Of Lord Rosebery the reverse would be more nearly true. He has the virtues of the cultivated few, and lacks the abilities that alone can reach the many.

1896.

MR. JOHN MORLEY

II

MR. JOHN MORLEY

MR. MORLEY'S interest to the observer is largely in his distinctness; for seldom is a man of importance so clear in outline until after his death, when time has wiped out details and placed the individual. Mr. Morley has no details; he has no blurred edges, no puzzles; he represents a familiar type, and he is distinct, partly for that reason, partly because he is expressive in words, but in a large degree because, since few men of his kind rise so high, he stands apart in the spectator's eye alike from other British statesmen and from other English critics. To gain a position of influence in politics, and to assure himself a place in criticism, without the aid of instinct for action, charm of style, personal magnetism, wit, or eloquence, he has certainly kept his gifts employed at a higher rate of interest than is earned by most men of as few talents. His somewhat limited field has been cultivated with a thoroughness that has brought a larger crop than many a richer and broader area. In the moralism where we find so readily the boundaries of his personality we must find also a partial explanation of his accomplishment. The difference between him and many other critics caged in the straitness of their convictions lies somewhat in his intellectual mistrust of many of the qualities which limit him, which leads him to avoid some of their worst results and to get out of them as much as they can do. His clear-headed scholarship gains much from this check of his perceptions on his instincts, and so does his statesmanship. Mr. Morley's dozen volumes have given him a settled rank as a critic who is valued by the scholar as highly as by the general reader; and this rank is due largely to his moral nature, to the ethical seriousness which in its extreme is his artistic failure, — to his moral nature, which made his attention loyal to a few large facts and principles, and helped him to give order to all of his studies, at whatever sacrifice of vivacity. His misfortune is that these principles are not timely, that they do not form a message needed and welcomed by the times, like that of Matthew Arnold, for instance, or that of Ruskin, and of course also because they are not set in a style of distinction, but rather in one soured by moralism and desiccated by science; so that the row of books stand on the shelf of the temporarily useful merely, read because they give certain information more intelligently than any other summary treatises now obtainable. "Historia quoquo modo scripta est semper legitur." Mr. Morley himself finds history always interesting. He handles large subjects with a sincerity and a dignity that testify to their importance.

Naturally such qualities show at their best in his larger books; and the lives of Diderot, Rousseau, and Cobden are almost satisfying. In the first two Mr. Morley has allowed the subjects themselves to supply the elements of vividness and beauty in generous quotations, while he himself showed judgment in marshalling the surrounding facts. In the life of Cobden he dealt with matters well within the scope of his mind and temperament, and no better work on the subject could be desired. The letters are connected by a narrative and comment written in their own spirit, which is Mr. Morley's in its general tone, while Cobden has the natural grasp of the concrete which Mr. Morley lacks, and lacks the power of abstraction which Mr. Morley has. In succinct narrative Mr. Morley is staccato and dry. He expands only in the region of the general, and there are consequently many dreary wastes in his political speeches which are rare in his books. In the life of Rousseau he scolds a little, but he lets the man paint himself, as he does Diderot, while he as editor tells the most important things which these men brought into the world. These three books are the truest foundation of the writer's interest for the world, however much more discussion arbitrary and radical arguments like those in " Compromise " may have aroused. The treatment may seem thin when we have read them all, but in reading them we can hardly fail to find constant food for the interest in serious principles of human progress which Pliny thought strong enough to make all history readable. They tell us almost nothing that is not worth knowing.

Another superiority of these longer works is that the author's faults are less insistent in them than in the shorter political and literary studies, to say nothing of the political speeches, which will hardly enter into the judgment of the future. The first of these faults or limitations is that in no degree is history a picture to Mr. Morley, — it is merely a problem. The past is not brought before the imagination, except in some quotations; it is only given, like a demonstration in geometry, to the eye of reason. He himself speaks in the life of Rousseau of "the greatest question that ever dawns upon any human intelligence that has the privilege of discerning it, the problem of a philosophy and body of doctrine." It is perhaps necessary to say of this judgment nothing more than that it is characteristic of its author not only in its sweeping generality but in its frank avowal of his own dominant interest. Mr. Morley has his own body of doctrine compact and unchanging, and other quotations will serve to show where it leads him. The scolding at religion; the irrelevant jeers, such as his suggestion that Hume's seasickness is probably a satisfaction to the orthodox; the famous small "g," the translation in Goethe's poem of "das uebrige Gott" by "the master power;" such violent speech inserted parenthetically as "the fatuous optimism which insists that somehow justice and virtue do rule in the world,"—these little offences against taste are obviously part of a larger limitation. The sharpness of his partisanship not only makes his speech bitter; it makes breadth and sympathy of imagination on some aspects of literature impossible to him, just as in some of his speeches he seems to have thrown away moderation and the critical attitude, and become the mere advocate, endeavoring to gain force by violence and persuasion by contempt. So far does his own panacea carry him that he makes for it claims that in one who has so fiercely pointed out the exaggerations of the claims of revealed religion and the slightness of the connection between belief and character are almost surprising: —

"A man with this faith can have no foul spiritual pride, for there is no mysteriously accorded divine grace in which one may be a larger participant than another; he can have no incentives to that mutilation with which every branch of the church, from the oldest to the youngest and crudest, has in its degree afflicted and retarded mankind, because the key-note of his religion is the joyful energy of every faculty, practical, reflective, creative, contemplative, in pursuit of a visible common good; and he can be plunged into no fatal and paralyzing despair by any doctrine of mortal sin, because active faith in humanity, resting on recorded experience, discloses the many possibilities of moral recovery, and the work that may be done for men in the fragment of days, redeeming the contrite from their burdens by manful hope."

A part of this philosophy or creed is his constant preaching, in season and out, that the social is the only worthy point of view, which naturally leads him to revel in the eighteenth century of France, since no period has had more greatness with less individuality, and no modern literature has as strong a social quality with such a dearth of original genius as the French. In his life of Diderot, Mr. Morley points out clearly how the particular sympathies of the great Frenchman in art and letters are the natural result of his social point of view,—his liking for Greuge, for instance, and for Richardson. The remarks which Mr. Morley interjects on every opportunity about the family relations make a rather picturesque, perhaps a diverting, commentary on similar results, less artistic to be sure, from his own emphatic social morality. In his Cobden is this judgment, in his sweeping manner: "the greatest of political morals, that 'domestic comfort is the object of all reforms.'" And in his Voltaire is this still more daring generalization: "To have really contributed in the humblest degree, for instance, to a peace between Prussia and her enemies in 1759, would have been an immeasurably greater performance for mankind than any given book which Voltaire could have written." From the same volume is an illustration which might be paralleled in almost any chapter Mr. Morley has written, for it is a belief so near his heart that it cannot be preached too much: "the general moral that active interest in public affairs is the only sure safeguard against the inhuman egotism, otherwise so nearly inevitable, and in anywise so revolting, of men of letters and men of science."

Obviously this absorption in ethical standards, in the directly social, leads Mr. Morley much farther than it could lead those more vivid imaginations which play freely and daringly with many aspects of the world; but it is hard to forbear giving one more example, because, detail though it is, it is so sharp an illustration that it is perhaps worth the space it takes. Everybody remembers with what scorn Mr. Morley attacked religious conformity, however quiet, in his treatise on compromise. Is it not almost ridiculous after pages of biting reproaches to those who, for one reason and another, deem it best to keep their belief to themselves, to find a passage telling us, in language which is its own comment on the effect of thought on style, in language which has at once the faults of the bar and those of that pulpit for which he has such a never silent contempt, of the one case in which we are not to act on the principles which he has been laying down:

"Where it would give them deep and sincere pain to hear a son or daughter avow disbelief in the inspiration of the Bible and so forth, it seems that the younger person is warranted in refraining from saying that he or she does not accept such and such doctrines. This, of course, only where the son or daughter feels a tender and genuine attachment to the parent. Where the parent has not earned this attachment, has been selfish, indifferent, or cruel, the title to the special kind of forbearance of which we are speaking can hardly exist. In an ordinary way, however, a parent has a claim on us which no other person in the world can have, and a man's self-respect ought scarcely to be injured if he finds himself shrinking from playing the apostle to his own father and mother.

"If a man drew his wife by lot, or by any other method over which neither he nor she has any control, as in the case of parents, perhaps he might with some plausibleness contend that he owed her certain limited deference and reserve, just as we admit that he may owe them to his parents. But such is not the case."

With this truly ingenuous doctrine of the wife compare this little piece of rhetoric: —

"The marriage choice of others is the inscrutable puzzle of those who have no eye for the fact that such choice is the great match of cajolery between purpose and invisible hazard, with the blessedness of many lives for stake, as intention happens to cheat accident or to be cheated by it. When the match is once over, deep criticism of a game of chance is time wasted."

It would hardly pay to go too deep into the conflicts of these two extracts, nor is deep search necessary to see in them some of the dangers into which the prophet who can give us solemn assurances in absolute form about the facts of our lives is likely to fall. Nothing, however, leads him into quite such impossible promulgations as these relations, which also lead him nearest to pure sentimentality in expression: —

"So sharp are the goads in a divided house; so sorely with ache and pain and deep-welling tears do men and women rend into shreds the fine web of one another's lives. But the pity of it, oh, the pity of it!"

It should be said, however, that this sensitiveness sometimes finds more pleasing expression: —

"It is the bitterest element in the vast irony of human life that the time-worn eyes to which a son's success would have brought the purest gladness are so often closed forever before success has come."

Evidently it is in such cases as these not the thing said so much as the way of saying it that makes the weakness. If Mr. Morley had more appreciation of beauty, even if he had not the gifts to express it, he would avoid some of his softest moralizations. His preference of the ethical to the æsthetic point of view is entirely conscious. "I like the drab men best;" and again: "Truth is quiet. . . . Moderation and judgment are, for most purposes, more than the flash and glitter even of the genius." The scientific and the ethical spirits have such complete possession of him that it is no wonder that when we read his Voltaire we see very little of the flash and glitter of the genius. "That he values knowledge only as a means to social action is one of the highest titles to our esteem that any philosopher can have." Then he has carried this line of thought so far that the definitions of art fixed by centuries of experience are undone to do homage to science: "tragedy to the modern is not *τύχη*, but a thing of cause and effect, invariable antecedent and invariable consquent." The present reaction against the excessive claims of science is not without its analogies to the reaction against the pretensions of revealed religion. Whatever tragedy may be to the fictitious individual here called the modern, invariable antecedent and invariable consequent have yet to justify themselves in the drama. In the novel they have done much, as they always have; but where is the play that has stood any test of time in which the point of view is not just the opposite, the strangeness of the powers that help or impede the course of man,— mystery, not the clearness of the scientific treatise? The wrongs done in the name of science have been no greater to religion than they have been to art and the criticism of art.

Not the least of the evil results of letting science out of bounds is its injury to language. Mr. Morley's large vocabulary, the result of wide reading in several languages, is made up indiscriminately of words that are formal and lifeless, and words that have real blood in them. His imagery shows the same influence. In the following passage from the essay on Condorcet the "less picturesquely" thrown in parenthetically from a mere passion for passing judgments is full of suggestion about the critic who threw it in; but the quotation is made especially to show the chilling anticlimax of the non-conducting metaphor after the pictures which preceded it.

"'Cordorcet,' said D'Alembert, 'is a volcano covered with snow.' Said another, less picturesquely, 'He is a sheep in a passion.' 'You may say of the intelligence of Condorcet in relation to his person,' wrote Madame Roland, 'that it is a subtle essence soaked in cotton.' The curious mixture disclosed, by sayings like these, of warm impulse and fine purpose with immovable reserve, only shows that he of whom they were spoken belonged to the class of natures which may be called non-conducting."

This lack of artistic feeling for language, which accompanies so naturally the cloud of moral judgments which checker all of Mr. Morley's writings, shows itself amusingly in single epithets. Turgot, whenever he is mentioned, however casually, is always "the great" or "the wise Turgot;" "justly," "admirably," "rightly," are constantly stuck on to quoted judgments, with no other effect than to destroy the charm; a swarm of things in the world happen "too often;" unpleasant words like "hateful" hover over the pages; if the laxities of genius are mentioned, the English nation is immediately dubbed with an unpleasant adjective for its supposed censures on the genius's conduct; "only partly true" is fastened like an icicle on to an interesting quotation,—and so on as long as one chose to continue the task of showing specifically the evil wrought in literary execution by the subordination of artistic to moral sensibility. Mr. Morley is well able to see this truth in others. "Macaulay's pages," he says, "are the record of sentences passed, not the presentation of human characters in all their fulness and color." The moralist has his excuse for being and for writing, but it is a commonplace that the laws of art apply to his work also.

One of the most curious manifestations of the moralistic spirit, more entertaining perhaps than displeasing, the confident dealing in superlatives, has already been mentioned, but the examples of it which Mr. Morley furnishes are so numerous and so extreme that the temptation to collect a few of them is irresistible. Voltaire is "the greatest worker that has ever lived," "the most graceful of all courtiers," and "the most trenchant writer in the world;" his letters "are wittier than any other letters in the world," and his Akakia is "the wittiest and most pitiless of all the purely personal satires in the world." Cicero is "the most eloquent of consuls or men," and Milton's Areopagitica is "the noblest defence that was ever made of the noblest of causes."

"The completeness of Catholicism as a self-containing system of life and thought is now harder for Protestants or Sceptics to realize than any other fact in the whole history of human society."

"These transformations of religion by leavening elements contributed from a foreign doctrine, are the most interesting process in the history of truth."

If we are tempted to ask what is the use of such infallibility, Mr. Morley can tell us by condemning the opposite, which he does, usually sarcastically, with a persistence equal to his untiring statement of universals. He speaks of "the marvellously multiplying beliefs of which we hear that they may be half right and half wrong;" and of "our lofty new idea of rational freedom as freedom from conviction, and of emanicipation of understanding as emancipation from the duty of settling whether important propositions are true or false." It is not necessary to decide whether that lofty ideal is new or older than Ecclesiastes, or whether or not it is wiser than its opposite, in order to dispose of the paradox sometimes put forward that Mr. Morley is at heart a Conservative, or of his own assertion that he is "a cautious Whig by temperament." Does he or the nation which he scolds come nearest to deserving this diatribe: —

"This inability to conceive of conduct except as either right or wrong, and, correspondingly in the intellectual order, of teaching except as either true or false, is at the bottom of that fatal spirit of *parti-pris* which has led to the noting of so much injustice, disorder, immobility, and darkness in English intelligence."

The greatest of these limitations, the lack of a message, is perhaps what justified his turning his strength from literature to politics, where his lack of beauty and of free play is a less absolute bar, where concentration and will can do more. The fixed principles without which he would never feel safe were required before he came near to concrete life, while he still saw things from afar; which marks him out clearly from the men whose principles seem to be imbibed unconsciously from the air about them, so that they become the spokesmen of some spirit of the time, changing often to express varying phases of the unseen forces that guide them. The far-reaching results in moulding issues, especially through his influence on a more creative personality, are known; but even in his steady onward march some of the same qualities that hold him back in literature show themselves. An American philosopher, in conversation, once spoke with enthusiasm of Mr.

Morley's character. "I do not understand your ardor," answered a Liberal statesman. "He is a very sensible man, but he is a pessimist." Even when Mr. Morley tells us cheerful things, he does not cheer us. There is something dreary about his pictures of improvements in the human lot. He has learned to talk more of good than of evil, but even when he scolds Mr. Lecky for pessimism there is something disheartening in his words of hope. That he should ever actually lead the nation is not easy to imagine, when we listen to a tone like this: —

> "It is the mark of the highest kind of union between sagacious, firm, and clear-sighted intelligence, and a warm and steadfast glow of feeling, when a man has learnt how little the effort of the individual can do either to hasten or direct the current of human destiny, and yet finds in effort his purest pleasure and his most constant duty. If we owe honor to that social endeavor which is stimulated and sustained by an enthusiastic confidence in speedy and full fruition, we surely owe it still more to those who, knowing how remote and precarious and long beyond their own days is the hour of fruit, yet need no other spur nor sustenance than bare hope, and in this strive and endeavor, and still endeavor. Here lies the true strength."

The moralizings of the man of action are short and occasional, and they are never reiterated complaints against the whole nation which they lead. One example of this nether side of the moralist spirit in Mr. Morley must suffice: —

"A community, in short, where the great aim of all classes and orders with power is, by dint of rigorous silence, fast shutting of the eyes, and stern stopping of the ears, somehow to keep the social pyramid on its apex, with the fatal result of preserving for England its glorious fame as a paradise for the well-to-do, a purgatory for the able, and a hell for the poor."

For the statesman who is content to take most of the faults of the nation and the race for granted, to offer no panacea but merely to do in a free spirit what seems best from day to day, Mr. Morley has still little respect, though more perhaps than he had when he spoke of "that sceptical and centrifugal state of mind which now tends to nullify organized liberalism and paralyze the spirit of improvement," which perhaps is not unlike his own in content, though with less storm and stress. Yet this very spirit, which takes the world artistically and serenely, often finds much to please it in the graceless but sterling combatant. Nobody of intelligence would fail to see Mr. Morley's attractions within the limitations of the species to which he belongs. His personality stands out as something real, something impressive. The same persistence that makes him talk forever against such fixed machinery as diplomacy, for instance, made him risk defeat to speak his belief on the eight-hour law. The faithfulness that made him thorough in his historical studies forced him into politics in middle life, because he could not preach one thing and do another. The declamation against book culture borrows a dignity when the declaimer bears up with such courage, after almost total failure, that he gains the ear of the nation. The world has one competent statesman more, and, instead of the hope that Mr. Morley's last literary work might surpass his first, it has the speeches and a few essays in which the old faults are missing, and with them the old virtues. There seems to be even less light in the struggle than at first; and the pursuit of the higher qualities of style is gone. Yet even from the literary standpoint we can hardly fail to be satisfied that he did what so few do, left his tastes to follow where his reason pointed. When we stand off and look at him in this generalized way, his faults are lost in the spectacle. The two characters of statesman and moralist, he has told us, "are always hard to reconcile, as perhaps any parliamentary candidate might tell us. The contrast between lofty writing and slippery policy has been too violent for Seneca's good fame, as it was for Francis Bacon's. It is ever at his own proper risk and peril that a man dares to present high ideals to the world." The inspiration for us in Mr. Morley's case is in the inconceivability of his failure to stand by his ideals. His arduous success marks out the superiority of the true scholar, who is not much out of place anywhere, while his parody the pedant, in Mr. Morley's own words, "cursed with the ambition to be a ruler of men, is a curious study. He would be glad not to go too far, and yet his chief dread is lest he be left behind. His consciousness of pure aims allows him to become an accomplice in the worst of crimes. Suspecting himself at bottom to be a theorist, he hastens to clear his character as a man of practice by conniving at an enormity." No rational person doubts that he is speaking in the tone that most truly represents his deepest feeling when he says: "There are causes that demand and deserve fury and energy and the public is to be got at upon no other terms,—say Anti-Slavery, or Reform; and men are properly adjured to strip off coat and waistcoat, charm or no charm." Certainly there is little of what is properly called charm, but a quality has developed itself gradually which perhaps comes nearer to it than anything else, — the tone of quiet sadness in which he sometimes sums up his new experiences, when he speaks of the failure of democracy to lead toward universal peace, or when he says: "It is one of the inscrutable perplexities of human affairs, that in the logic of practical life, in order to reach conclusions that cover enough for truth, we are constantly driven to premises that cover too much, and that in order to secure their right weight to justice and reason, good men are forced to fling the two-edged sword of passion into the same scale."

John Morley's fanaticism, wrote James Russell Lowell, "is always exhilarating to me, though I feel that it would have the same placidly convinced expression if my head were rolling at his feet at the exigence of some principle." That judgment certainly strikes the key-note. Although lack of art or genius has followed Mr. Morley from letters into politics, although his love of absolute principle is in opposition to the spirit of a time that has no creed, the persistence which has helped him to escape failure and the straightness of his course make a picture that has some of the stimulus of the heroic. In spite of the distinctness of his qualities, their relative importance changes so readily with the mood of the observer that it is not easy to keep together appreciation of his worth and understanding of his limits. Lowell, by the humorous choice of words, has been able to suggest the amusing in naming the impressive. On the one hand is the man whose writing is full of the perversities of the dogmatist and the closet philosopher, whose statesmanship lacks instinct and sensitiveness to facts that are too complex for statement, whose whole spirit seems thin and quarrelsome; and on the other hand is the serious and rather sad thinker who has measured himself without vanity and taken the harder path from a sense of duty, who thinks he sees some changes that will make men happier, and who follows them without fear; who took up his new fight not to complete his own experience but to obey that truth which exists for him in a more tangible and discernible, and perhaps in a more limited form than it does for most men of his size in our generation.

1897.

MR. BALFOUR SEEN FROM A DISTANCE

III

MR. BALFOUR SEEN FROM A DISTANCE

ALTHOUGH it is difficult to judge fairly from his books alone a man whose activity has taken many forms, the proverb that the style is the man is not an empty phrase. What the written words tell us is truth, though often not the whole truth. Though the traits picked out of the expression of abstract thought may not be the traits that would be prominent in the same man in action, in his social or political environment, they may be none the less intimately an outline of the whole personality. Many persons who have no opportunity to watch Mr. Balfour in Parliament, in society, in recreation; no opportunity to know the facts of his early training and of his present life, have by necessity been driven, when they wished to make more definite their idea of the picturesque young leader, to pick up suggestions in his books; and of these many persons, a number get less from examining technically his system of philosophy than they do from looking with some minuteness at his habits of expression.

To many a college student in America the name of A. J. Balfour, which he discovers on the shelves of the Department of Philosophy, is almost unknown. By a class of students which is in our larger universities considerable in size, the discovery of a "Defence of Philosophic Doubt" is almost invariably welcomed with enthusiasm, as doubtless hereafter his later and more popular book will be welcomed. The young student whose love of logic has made him a personal enemy of some of the present scientists is delighted at the trenchant style in which his newly discovered ally attacks the inconsistencies of the leaders of thought. Mr. Balfour does not make converts, but he gives welcome weapons to thinkers whose attitude is the same and whose strength is less. The young metaphysician who has not been able to crystallize his prejudice into a critical system finds in the books of Mr. Balfour much help in stating reasons for his rejection of the various systems of philosophy, and thus, being able to accomplish that necessary work, he is able, if other things are in him, to go on more quickly. "If speculations which do nothing but destroy seem to be, as indeed they are, unsatisfactory even from a practical point of view," says Mr. Balfour in "A Defence of Philosophic Doubt," "the reader must recollect that definite and rational certainty is not likely to be obtained unless we first pass through a stage of definite and rational doubt."

A rational certainty, however, though it may be a good we get from Mr. Balfour, is not the one we go to him for. His readers, far from seeking the removal of difficulties, revel in them. The attraction is less in the final result of his thought than in the adroitness with which he exposes inconsistency in established thought. Naturally a youth of logical and critical bent, who has become irritated at the deference shown to men of more fertility than coherence, revels in a passage like this: —

"Looking back over the nineteen chapters we have been considering, and over the earlier half of the 'First Principles,' it is impossible not to regret that the ambition to produce a 'System of Philosophy' should have forced our author into paths where his remarkable powers of mind show to comparatively small advantage. Could he have been content with giving to the world 'Suggestions toward a Theory of the Universe on the Basis of the Ordinary Scientific Postulates,' his astonishing faculty for collecting from every department of knowledge the facts which seem to tell in his favor would have had free scope, while his somewhat blunted sensibilities in the matter of difficulties and contradictions might have been of actual advantage. In trespassing on metaphysical grounds, the virtues which he possesses as a thinker — his extraordinary range of information and his ingenuity in framing original and suggestive hypotheses — become comparatively useless, while the robust faith in his methods and results by which he is animated — necessary as I admit it to be in order that he may be sustained through his protracted labors — is from a speculative point of view an almost unmixed evil."

Certainly such cutting summaries, in which he seems to rejoice in a vocabulary fitted to his critical acuteness, are from an artistic standpoint the best things he does. This, like his other powers, is more obvious than his defects, and it may be for this reason, as well as for the purpose of exhibiting an easy magnanimity, that the many reviewers who have attacked his results have passed off his literary qualities with a few words of praise. Yet the defects of his style, though less salient, are as undeniable as its merits. Indeed, in literary skill he is often so deficient as to surprise the reader who has a taste for close examination.

Perhaps Mr. Balfour's highest literary merits may be roughly summarized as subtlety and originality. It is his subtlety in analysis that makes his satire, whether or not it is backed by conclusive arguments, go for a point at which it will hurt, and where it will be difficult to parry. Although it is, for instance, possible to believe that there is progress in human understanding, and that this belief is final and needs no support, it is not easy, in reading the following dialogue, to avoid the feeling that the scientist is involved in a fallacy: —

"*Evolutionist:* However great the superiority of my views may be over those of my remote ancestors, or, indeed, over those of my contemporaries who are still under the influence of tradition, there is every reason to suppose that the causes which have produced this superiority are still in operation, and that we may look forward to a time when the opinions of mankind will bear the same relation to ours as ours bear to those of primitive man.

"*Inquirer:* A glorious hope! One, nevertheless, which would seem to imply that many of our present views are either entirely wrong, or will require profound modification.

"*Evolutionist:* Doubtless.

"*Inquirer:* It would be interesting to know *which* of our opinions, or which class of them, is likely to be improved in this way off the face of the earth.

For example, is the opinion you have just expressed, that beliefs are developed according to law, — is that opinion likely to be destroyed by development?"

Of course Mr. Balfour himself is not confused. No one knows better than he that, as some beliefs must be final, it is possible, with clearness at least, to take one's final stand on a belief in human progress. To say that progress may remove the belief in progress is simply to express a disagreement with the final assumption. It is like disagreeing with Mr. Balfour's belief in God. He believes in God because the belief unifies a number of other beliefs which, for working purposes, he wishes to hold. The scientist's belief in progress has the same foundation.

Although, however, Mr. Balfour can thus use his subtlety in support of an argument known by him to be unsound, he is even stronger in expression when he supports principles in which he believes. To say that these principles are negative is not to suggest any dislike of them. When the author's strong tastes are attacked as unprogressive, he resents the attack with a *tu quoque* argument of such vividness that it comes nearer than anything else in his books to emotional power. Sometimes the thrust is delicate, as in this reference to Matthew Arnold's substitute for the established faith: —

"There are those, again, who reject in its ordinary shape the idea of divine superintendence, but who conceive that they can escape from philosophic reproach by beating out the idea yet a little thinner, and admitting that there does exist somewhere a 'power which makes for righteousness.'"

Sometimes it is rough, even crude, especially when he speaks of the positivists: —

"Mr. Spencer, who pierces the future with a surer gauge than I can make the least pretence to, looks confidently forward to a time when the relation of man to his surroundings will be so happily contrived that the reign of absolute righteousness will prevail; conscience, grown unnecessary, will be dispensed with; the path of least resistance will be the path of virtue; and not the 'broad' but the 'narrow way' will 'lead to destruction.' These excellent consequences seem to me to flow very smoothly and satisfactorily from his particular doctrine of evolution, combined with his particular doctrine of morals. But I confess that my own personal gratification at the prospect is somewhat dimmed by the reflection that the same kind of causes which make conscience superfluous will relieve us from the necessity of intellectual effort, and that by the time we are all perfectly good we shall also be all perfectly idiotic."

The insertion of such sign-posts of irony as "excellent" consequences, "his particular" doctrine, and the pretentious final phrase which covers the venerable contention that the struggle with evil is necessary for intelligent life, is characteristic of his rougher satire. Though the satire is rather refreshing, even to one who laughs at it rather than at its object, it is hardly dignified, and it is a contrast to the style in which he expresses, with no enemy in mind, his own beliefs.

Critics of his philosophy often assert that he has no beliefs. They charge him with insincerity, and attempt to prove the charge by showing him stating at one time one truth and at another its opposite. It is undoubtedly easy to bring together passages on both sides of all of the philosophic controversies which he discusses. A striking contrast, for instance, might be made between his pictures of the bad effects of the over emphasis of science, and his explanations of the absolute impossibility of knowing what present tendencies are for good and what for bad. It is no cause for wonder that some readers feel an inconsistency between the author's confident statements of the ultimate results that will follow from certain beliefs or from certain failures to believe, and such a passage as this: —

"The ceaseless conflict, the strange echoes of long-forgotten controversies, the confusion of purpose, the success in which lay deep the seeds of future evils, the failures that ultimately divert the otherwise inevitable danger, the heroism which struggles to the last for a cause predoomed to defeat, the wickedness which sides with right, and the wisdom which huzzas with the triumph of folly, — fate, meanwhile, amidst this turmoil and perplexity, working silently towards the predestined end, — all these form together a subject the contemplation of which need surely never weary."

Why, then, one might well ask, may we not look at the confused efforts of the scientist as an interesting part of this incalculable spectacle, instead of quarrelling with him over some immediate consequences that we think bad? Of course the answer is really simple. Consistency, to quote Emerson, is a vice of small minds. The fact that Mr. Balfour's arguments do not all pull in the same direction is not an argument against, but for his sincerity. His desires and his beliefs are various. He likes to use his acuteness in pointing out the incongruities in the creeds of others, and he is aware, also, of the flaws in his own doctrines, although, as part of the game, he protects as well as he can the vulnerable points in his own creed. His insincerity is superficial. He is perfectly frank with himself. That he knows that his own vulnerable points are much like those of his adversaries, and covers this fact for forensic purposes, is no reason to doubt his earnestness. Though the talk occasionally made about his ardent faith by the orthodox persons whom he supports is somewhat absurd, he has a strong sincerity of his own sceptical kind, — a sincerity as strong as that of any of his positivist opponents, and to one seeking the incongruous equally grotesque. Sincerity as a matter of temperament, of general attitude toward life, he has in abundance. Life to him is serious in a high degree. With any detail of it, a religion, a personality, a science, he deals lightly in some moods; but toward existence as a whole he is never flippant; through all his doubt and satire is a genuine sense of wonder, interest, and ignorance, a feeling of the complexity and awfulness of life, — the feeling that gives dignity to the ablest sceptics. One feels this less in single passages than in the books as a whole. The reason for this is that Mr. Balfour's single passages usually show more his weakness than his strength. However, this sense of wonder, resignation, and powerlessness is frequently shown, sometimes with rhetoric, sometimes simply. It is seen less convincingly in his direct exhortations and statements of belief than in indirect ways, such as his tone in his appreciations of character, — especially his appreciation of noble men engaged in futile efforts. In such estimates, where it is not the fighter but the man of taste who speaks, his style loses its crudity, and gains a warmth and simplicity that touch the feelings and gain the approval of the reader who can take in the flights of militant rhetoric only an ironical interest. This side of Mr. Balfour is in the last part of this passage from his latest book:

"Metaphysicians are poets who deal with the abstract and the supersensible instead of the concrete and the sensuous. To be sure, they are poets with a difference. Their appropriate and characteristic gifts are not the vivid realization of that which is given in experience; their genius does not prolong, as it were, and echo through the remotest regions of feeling the shock of some definite emotion; they create for us no new worlds of things and persons; nor can it be often said that the product of their labors is a thing of beauty. . . . Yet, in spite of all this, they can only be justly estimated by those who are prepared to apply to them a quasi-æsthetic standard. . . . For claims to our admiration will still be found in their brilliant intuitions, in the subtlety of their occasional arguments, in their passion for the Universal and the Abiding, in their steadfast faith in the rationality of the world, in the devotion with which they are content to live and move in realms of abstract speculation too far removed from ordinary interests to excite the slightest sympathy in the breasts even of the cultivated few."

This passage illustrates what I called his second power, originality. He has generally most originality where he has least obvious subtlety. Originality in this sense is directness of thought, freshness of point of view, individuality. To be original, said Goethe, is to say and do, as though it had never been done before, what many say and do every day. It is in his tastes, his enjoyments, and his sympathies, that Mr. Balfour shows most of this individual thought and feeling. The sympathetic picture of the metaphysician illustrates it. It is illustrated also, for instance, in his sympathy with the average man's motiveless curiosity. Of the many men who recognize that the consequences of an interest are not the only standard of appreciation, that there is the direct æsthetic standard also, few give an expression to these immediate values of more convincing sincerity than the expression of Mr. Balfour: —

"We hear much of what is called 'idle curiosity,' but I am loath to brand any form of curiosity as necessarily idle. Take, for example, one of the most singular, but in this age one of the most universal, forms in which it is accustomed to manifest itself, — I mean that of an exhaustive study of the morning and evening papers. It is certainly remarkable that any person who has nothing to get by it should destroy his eyesight and confuse his brain by a conscientious attempt to master the dull and doubtful details of the European diary daily transmitted to us by 'Our Special Correspondent.' But it must be remembered that this is only a somewhat unprofitable exercise of that disinterested love of knowledge which moves men to penetrate Polar snows, to build up systems of philosophy, or to explore the secrets of the remotest heavens. . . . I admit, of course, at once that discoveries the most apparently remote from human concerns have often proved themselves of the utmost commercial or manufacturing value. But they require no such justification for their existence, nor were they striven for with any such object."

This sympathy with a thing for itself, not for its consequences, is the one element of imagination that Mr. Balfour has. He lacks the creative, the expressive elements. He cannot give life to a character sketch, or passion to an argument, although his sympathy with the logic of many points of view is keen. "Argument is all I have to offer," he says in closing his "Defence of Philosophic Doubt."

The phrase has the sound of grave resignation to a limitation. His arguments sometimes make us feel that the author has warmth, conviction, sympathy. The warmth is for many things, excessive for none; the conviction is of the absolute values of certain temperaments and attitudes, apart from any outside standard of worth; the sympathy is with the rational essence of a character, not with its details, its concrete embodiment. This personality, lacking as it is in brilliant colors, is one for which it is possible to have strong affection and deep respect, for it is earnest and it is individual. One may care little for Mr. Balfour's skilful force, and much for his breadth of sympathy and for the first-hand quality of his thought.

The happiest illustrations of his personality in his style are in homely similes: —

> "Do they follow, I mean, on reason *qua* reason, or are they, like a schoolboy's tears over a proposition of Euclid, consequences of reasoning, but not conclusions from it?"

This is Mr. Balfour at his best, exact, ready, at once harmonious and grave, with a simplicity of illustration well suited to his subtlety of distinction: —

> ". . . the right of every individual to judge for himself is like the right of every man who possesses

a balance at his banker's to require its immediate payment in sovereigns. The right may be undoubted, but it can only be safely enjoyed on condition that too many persons do not take it into their heads to exercise it together."

Sometimes, though less often, there is the same felicity in his more serious, or rather more solemn, expressions. The felicity is naturally rarer in expressing moods that are taken with effort. Religion, in the sense in which he defends it, is not an emotion with Mr. Balfour. He has not even a feeling of congeniality and companionship with it. He is only its protector. It is religion as a branch of æsthetics, and religion as a conclusion of logic, that are spontaneous interests for him. When he takes a high, solemn tone about it, he is flowery and stilted. It is when he talks with his native ease and irony that his freshness, urbanity, and clearness appear: —

"We do not, for example, step over a precipice because we are dissatisfied with all the attempts to account for gravitation. In theology, however, experience does lean too timidly on theory. . . . Because they cannot contrive to their satisfaction a system of theological jurisprudence which shall include Redemption as a leading case, Redemption is no longer to be counted among the consolations of mankind."

Mr. Balfour is, then, at his best remarkably keen, apt, simple, and individual. Of the faults to be set opposite these merits the largest is effort. Not only is the argument often perfunctory and dry, but the rhetoric with which it is supported is forced and flat. Perhaps a satisfactory proof of this is in the last half of a passage which has been praised more than any other Mr. Balfour has written: —

> "Man, so far as natural science by itself is able to teach us, is no longer the final cause of the universe, the heaven-descended heir of all the ages. His very existence is an accident, his story a brief and transitory episode in the life of one of the meanest of the planets. Of the combination of causes which first converted a dead organic compound into the living progenitors of humanity, science, indeed, as yet knows nothing. It is enough that from such beginnings famine, disease, and mutual slaughter, fit nurses of the future lords of creation, have gradually evolved, after infinite travail, a race with conscience enough to feel that it is vile, and intelligence enough to know that it is insignificant. We survey the past, and see that its history is of blood and tears, of helpless blundering, of wild revolt, of stupid acquiescence, of empty aspirations."

One of the most striking examples of his weak efforts for literary effect is in the middle of one of his most interesting passages. In speaking of Handel he is trying to suggest a quality, "the one most valued in modern art," which Handel lacks: —

> "Pathos hardly renders it; for though it can hardly be cheerful, it need be impregnated with no more than the faintest and most luxurious flavor of melancholy. There is in it something indirect, ambiguous, complex."

Thus far all is well; but now comes an absurd statement absurdly illustrated: "Though in itself positive enough, it is, perhaps, most easily described by negatives. It is not grief, nor joy, nor despair, nor merriment." Obviously the statement that it is best described by negatives is put in to introduce the string of words in the next sentence. To say that this vague melancholy is not grief is well enough; it is not altogether absurd to say that it is not despair; but the statement that it is not joy or merriment is born of the desire to make a sounding sentence. The rest of the exposition is done more intelligently: —

> "It is no simple emotion struck direct out of the heart by the shock of some great calamity or some unlooked for good fortune. If it suggests, as it often does, an unsatisfied longing, it is a longing vague and far off, which reaches toward no defined

or concrete object. It is the product and the delight of a highly-wrought civilization, but of a civilization restless and tormented, neither contented with its destiny nor at peace with itself."

In beginning the explanation, Mr. Balfour thus prefaced his way: —

"To describe this with accuracy, nay, to describe it at all, is scarcely possible. Even to indicate vaguely its nature is not easy; since music, not literature, has been its chief exponent, and for these fine shades of sentiment language scarcely provides a terminology of sufficient delicacy and precision."

It may make vivid Mr. Balfour's entire lack of strong and simple strokes in any writing but the ironical or the purely logical to compare all this mixture of sense and nonsense with a few words on the same subject from Turgenieff's "Fathers and Sons": —

"But since I have just pronounced this word 'happiness,' I must ask you a question. Why, even when we enjoy music, for example, a fine evening, or a conversation with one who sympathizes with us, — why does the enjoyment appear to us an allusion to some unknown happiness to be found somewhere else, much rather than real happiness, a happiness that we are ourselves enjoying? Answer me. . . ."

Taken even more in detail, Mr. Balfour's style shows a similar lack of firmness. To one who knows his history before he reads his books, it is a surprise to find ineffective words, faults of grammar, and awkward constructions in his style. Not only his known interest in literature, but the quality of his thought when he analyzes politics, ethics, or persons, would lead one to expect from him an instinct for the structure of language, its technique. Yet his pages are full of the most elementary mistakes. These things are the more surprising that his style suggests much care and revision. This shows how little instinct he has for form in writing. There seems to be only one of the grammatical errors that usually come from a lack of literary training that he avoids. He never uses the split infinitive. As this error, though less awkward and illogical than the mistakes Mr. Balfour makes constantly, has been more discussed, his avoidance of it shows that he is willing to write correctly when he is told how, but that he is himself without the instinct.

Allied to his incorrectness in construction is a use of superfluous and weakening words. It is almost grotesque to find an explanatory "rightly," "fortunately," or "unhappily," wherever it can possibly be inserted. The frequent underscorings, and the absurdly numerous superlatives, are other similar weaknesses in his style. He seldom speaks long of any one without giving him a superlative of some kind.

It is, perhaps, useless to argue that a multitude of small weaknesses of this kind have a marked effect on the power of the style as a whole. It is certainly seldom that a man so keen in criticism and so familiar with all the arts has had so few of the technical merits and so many of the elementary faults of style. His sentences have none of the architectural elements of style. There is no force, no charm gained by the sound or the rhythm, no sonority or majesty. Therefore, there is no emotional force in Mr. Balfour's language, and no artistic attraction. It is awkward, jerky, inaccurate, and inelegant. Of course it would be easy to deduce too much from this entire lack of taste in composition. It would hardly lead to truth to use the qualities of Mr. Balfour's style so radically as he himself uses the style of another writer: —

"Shaftesbury is not, to me at least, an attractive writer. His constant efforts to figure simultaneously as a fine gentleman and a fine writer are exceedingly irritating; and the very moderate success which attended his efforts in the latter character suggests the doubt, justified by his later style, whether he can really have shone in the former."

Of course that is absurd. Shaftesbury may or may not have been a fine gentleman, however little relation there was between the pretensions and the actual value of his style. Mr. Balfour is certainly a man of the best taste in some ways; and the fact that he sometimes produces bombast, when he attempts to produce eloquence, is but a proof that his critical power, keen as it is, is limited in its range. Perhaps the most general judgment one draws from Mr. Balfour's style is that what there is of the author is attractive, but that the personality is not a very large one. He says of Berkeley:—

"Berkeley's early work is distinguished not only by the admirable qualities of originality, lucidity, and subtlety, but by a less excellent characteristic, which I can only describe as a certain *thinness* of treatment. At the time when he produced these immortal speculations he had read little and felt little. No experience of the weary entanglements of concrete facts had yet suggested to him that a perfect solution of the problem of the universe is beyond our reach."

Mr. Balfour has seen the difficulties of facts, and he has read a good deal, but of the kind of emotion that makes strong literature he has known nothing. Like Berkeley's early work, his books are original, lucid, subtle, and rather thin.

When Mr. Balfour's political career began we used to read ironical criticisms of him as a *dilettante*, a literary man, a youth without vigor, loving music and art, incapable of stern practical work. He has now proved that it is in practical activity that his strength lies. His importance is neither in literature nor in philosophy, but in the field from which his tastes seemed at one time farthest removed. He has the power of dealing with the complex facts, guided partly by general theories, partly by instinct, — a power more interesting in him than in most statesmen, because there are few successful men of action who understand the instincts on which they act as well as Mr. Balfour understands his. He puts into practical politics a subtler, broader, more complicated intelligence than is usually found there, — a thorough scepticism, combined with thorough earnestness. His beliefs and his doubts alike strengthen him in this branch of his activity, though they are not beliefs and doubts that form a great style or a great philosophy. He is an object of uncommon interest to many to-day, not because he is remarkable as a writer, a philosopher, an aristocrat, or a *dilettante*, but because he has become strong in political action, with no loss of his less practical interests. It is a rather singular figure that rises out of his books, — a character of much fineness and force, with general, broad fairness mixed with some strong prejudices; a mind without exuberant powers, though with rare keenness, interested always, and never excited. It is a mind of logic primarily, with little passion or sense of form. It is probably altogether a combination that exists seldom, if ever, outside of England, where the power of action has more often than elsewhere been combined with the temperament that looks out on the world as a panorama. It is in England that we see most often the uncompromising critic of the final ends of life in the man who has the keenest taste for the battles about him, and the combination has seldom been seen in so striking a form as it can be seen in Mr. Balfour.

1895.

STENDHAL

IV

STENDHAL

The fact that none of his work has been translated into English is probably a source of amused satisfaction to many of the lovers of Beyle. Though he exercised a marked influence on Mérimée, was wildly praised by Balzac, was discussed twice by Sainte-Beuve, was pointed to in Maupassant's famous manifesto-preface to "Pierre et Jean;" though he has been twice eulogized by Taine, and once by Bourget; and though he has been carefully analyzed by Zola, — he is read little in France, and scarcely at all elsewhere. While his name, at his death scarcely heard beyond his little circle of men of letters, has become rather prominent, his books are still known to very few. His cool prophecy that a few leading spirits would read him by 1880 was justified, and the solution of his doubt whether he would not by 1930 have sunk again into oblivion seems now at least as likely as it was then to be an affirmative. "To the happy few" he dedicated his latest important novel, and it will be as it has been for the few, happy in some meanings of that intangible word, that his character and his writings have a serious interest.

In one of the "Edinburgh Review's" essays on Mme. du Deffand is a rather striking passage in which Jeffrey sums up the conditions that made conversation so fascinating in the salons of the France of Louis XV. In "Rome, Florence, et Naples," published shortly afterwards by Beyle under his most familiar pseudonym of "Stendhal," is a conversation, with all the marks of a piece of genuine evidence on the English character, between the author and an Englishman; and yet a large part of what is given as the opinion of this acquaintance of Beyle is almost a literal translation of Jeffrey's remarks on the conditions of good conversation. Such a striking phrase as "Where all are noble all are free" is taken without change, and the whole is stolen with almost equal thoroughness. This trait runs through all of his books. He was not a scholar, so he stole his facts and many of his opinions, with no acknowledgments, and made very pleasing books.

Related, perhaps, to this quality, are the inexactness of his facts and the unreliability of his judgments. Berlioz, somewhere in his memoirs, gives to Stendhal half a dozen lines, which run something like this:—

> "There was present also one M. Beyle, a short man, with an enormous belly, and an expression which he tries to make benign and succeeds in making malicious. He is the author of a 'Life of Rossini,' full of painful stupidities about music."

Painful indeed, to a critic with the enthusiasm and the mastery of Berlioz, a lot of emphatic judgments from a man who was ignorant of the technique of music, who took it seriously but lazily, and who could make such a comment at the end of a comparison of skill with inspiration, as, "What would not Beethoven do, if, with his technical knowledge, he had the ideas of Rossini?" Imagine the passionate lover of the noblest in music hearing distinctions drawn between form and idea in music, with condescension for Beethoven, by a man who found his happiness in Cimarosa and Rossini. Imagine Beyle talking of grace, sweetness, softness, voluptuousness, ease, tune, and Berlioz running away to hide from these effeminate notions in Beethoven's harmonies! Imagine them crossing over into literature and coming there at the height to the same name, — Shakespeare! What different Shakespeares they are! Berlioz, entranced, losing self-control, feeling with passion the glowing life of the poet's words, would turn, as from something unclean, from the man whose love for Macbeth showed itself mostly in the citation of passages that give fineness to the feelings which the school of Racine thought unsuited to poetry. "You use it as a thesis," the enthusiast might cry. "The grandeur, the wealth, the terror of it, escape you. You see his delicacy, his proportion, a deeper taste than the classic French taste, and it forges you a weapon. But you are not swept on by him, you never get into the torrent, you are cool and shallow, and your praise is profanation." Stendhal read Shakespeare with some direct pleasure, no doubt, but he was always on the look-out for quotations to prove some thesis; and he read Scott and Richardson, probably all the books he read in any language, in the same unabandoned, restricted way.

In painting it is the same. It is with

a narrow and *dilettante* intelligence that he judges pictures. The painter who feeds certain sentiments, he loves and thinks great. Guido Reni is suave; therefore only one or two in the world's history can compare with him. One of them is Correggio, for his true voluptuousness. These are the artists he loves. Others he must praise, as he praised Shakespeare, to support some attack on French canons of art; therefore is Michelangelo one of the gods. The effort is apparent throughout; and as he recalls the fact that Mme. du Deffand and Voltaire saw in Michelangelo nothing but ugliness, and notes that such is the attitude of all true Frenchmen, the lover of Beyle smiles at his effort to get far enough away from his own saturated French nature to love the masculine and august painter he is praising. Before the Moses, Mérimée tells us, Beyle could find nothing to say beyond the observation that ferocity could not be better depicted. This vague, untechnical point of view was no subject of regret to Stendhal. He gloried in it. "Foolish as a scholar," he says somewhere; and in another place, "Vinci is a great artist, precisely because he is no scholar."

Add to lack of truthfulness, lack of thoroughness and lack of imagination, a total disregard for any moral view of life,—in the sense of a believing, strenuous view,—and you have, from the negative side, the general aspects of Stendhal's character. He was not vicious,—far from it,—though he admires many things that are vicious. He is not indecent, for "the greatest enemy of voluptuousness is indecency," and voluptuousness tests all things. The keen Duclos has said that the French are the only people among whom it is possible for the morals to be depraved without either the heart being depraved or the courage being weakened. It would be almost unfair to speak of Beyle's morals as depraved, as even in his earliest childhood he seems to have been without a touch of any moral quality. "Who knows that the world will last a week?" he asks, and the question expresses well the instinct in him that made him deny any appeal but that of his own ends. Both morals and religion really repel him. It is impossible to love a supreme being, he says, though we may perhaps respect him. Indeed, he believes that love and respect never go together,—that grace, which he loves, excludes force, which he respects; and thus he loves Reni and respects Michelangelo. Grace and force are the opposite sides of a sphere, and the human eye cannot see both. As for him, he fearlessly takes sympathy and grace and abandons nobility. In the same manner that he excludes strenuous feelings of right altogether, he makes painting, which he thinks the nobler art, secondary to music, which is the more comfortable. For a very sensitive man, he goes on, with real coherence to the mind of a Beylian, painting is only a friend, while music is a mistress. Happy indeed he who has both friend and mistress. In some of his moods the more austere, the nobler and less personal tastes and virtues, interest him, for he is to some extent interested in everything; but except where he is supporting one of his few fundamental theses, he does not deceive himself into thinking he likes them, and he never takes with real seriousness anything he does not like. Elevation and ferocity are the two words he uses over and over again in explaining that Michelangelo alone could paint the Bible; and the very poverty of his vocabulary, so discriminating when he is on more congenial subjects, suggests how external was the acquaintance of Beyle with elevation or ferocity, with Michelangelo or the Bible.

He has written entertainingly on such subjects, but it all has the sound of guesswork. These two qualities, with which he sums up the sterner aspects of life, are perhaps not altogether separable from a third, — dignity; and his view of this last may throw some light on the nature of his relations with the elevation and ferocity he praises. Here is a passage from "Le Rouge et le Noir": "Mathilde thought she saw happiness. This sight, all-powerful with people who combine courageous souls with superior minds, had to fight long against dignity and all vulgar sentiments of duty." Equally lofty is his tone towards other qualities that are in reality part of the same attitude, — a tone less of reproach than of simple contempt. The heroine of "Le Rouge et le Noir" is made to argue that "it is necessary to return in good faith to the vulgar ideas of purity and honor." Two more of the social virtues are disposed of by him in one extract, which, by the way, illustrates also the truly logical and the apparently illogical nature of Stendhal's thought. It will take a little reflection to see how he gets so suddenly from industry to patriotism in the following judgment, but the coherence of the thought will be complete to the Beylian: —

"It is rare that a young Neapolitan of fourteen is forced to do anything disagreeable. All his life he prefers the pain of want to the pain of work. The fools from the North treat as barbarians the citizens of this country, because they are not unhappy at wearing a shabby coat. Nothing would seem more laughable to an inhabitant of Crotona than to suggest his fighting to get a red ribbon in his buttonhole, or to have a sovereign named Ferdinand or William. The sentiment of loyalty, or devotion to dynasty, which shines in the novels of Sir Walter Scott, and which should have made him a peer, is as unknown here as snow in May. To tell the truth, I don't see that this proves these people fools. (I admit that this idea is in very bad taste.)"

For himself, he hated his country, as he curtly puts it, and loved none of his relatives. Patriotism, for which his contempt is perhaps mixed with real hatred, is in his mind allied to the worst of all stupid tyrants, propriety, or, as he more often calls it, opinion, his most violent aversion. Napoleon, he thinks, in destroying the custom of *cavaliere serviente*, simply added to the world's mass of *ennui* by ushering into Italy the flat religion of propriety. He is full of such lucid observations as that the trouble with opinion is that it takes a hand in private matters, whence comes the sadness of England and America. To this sadness of the moral countries and the moral people he never tires of referring. His thesis carries him so far that he bunches together Veronese and Tintoretto under the phrase, "painters without ideal," in whom there is something dry, narrow, reasonable, bound by propriety; in a word, incapable of rapture. This referring to some general standard, this lack of directness, of fervor, of abandonment, is illustrated by the Englishman's praise of his mistress, that there was nothing vulgar in her. It would take, Beyle says, eight days to explain that to a Milanese, and then he would have a fit of laughter.

These few references illustrate fairly the instincts and beliefs that are the basis of Stendhal's whole thought and life. The absolute degree of moral scepticism that is needed to make a sympathetic reader of him is — especially among people refined and cultivated enough to care for his subjects — everywhere rare. I call it a moral rather than an intellectual scepticism, because, while he would doubtless deny the possibility of knowing the best good of the greatest number, a more ultimate truth is that he is perfectly indifferent to the good of the greatest number. It is unabashed egotism. The assertion of his individual will, absolute loyalty to his private tastes, is his principle of thought and action, and his will and his tastes do not include the rest of the world and its desires: —

"What is the ME? I know nothing about it. One day I awoke upon this earth; I found myself united to a certain body, a certain fortune. Shall I go into the vain amusement of wishing to change them, and in the mean time forget to live? That is to be a dupe. I submit to their failings. I submit to my aristocratic bent, after having declaimed for ten years, in good faith, against all aristocracy. I adore Roman noses, and yet, if I am a Frenchman, I resign myself to having received from heaven only a Champagne nose: what can I do about it? The Romans were a great evil for humanity, a deadly disease which retarded the civilization of the world. . . . In spite of so many wrongs, my heart is for the Romans."

Thus, in all the details of his extended comparison, Beyle tries to state with fairness the two sides, — the general good and the personal, the need of obedience to its rules if some general ends of society are to be attained, and the individual's loss from obedience. He states with fairness, but his own choice is never in doubt. He goes to what directly pleases him:—

"Shall I dare to talk of the bases of morals? From the accounts of my comrades I believe that there are as many deceived husbands at Paris as at Boulogne, at Berlin as at Rome. The whole difference is that at Paris the sin is caused by vanity, and at Rome by climate. The only exception I find is in the middle classes in England, and all classes at Geneva. But, upon my honor, the drawback in *ennui* is too great. I prefer Paris. It is gay."

His tastes, his sympathies, are unhesitatingly with the Roman in the following judgment:—

"A Roman to whom you should propose to love always the same woman, were she an angel, would exclaim that you were taking from him three quarters of what makes life worth while. Thus, at Edinburgh, the family is first, and at Rome it is a detail. If the system of the Northern people sometimes begets the monotony and the *ennui* that we read on their faces, it often causes a calm and continuous happiness."

This steady contrast is noted by his mind merely, his logical fairness. His mind is judicial in a sort of negative, formal sense; judicial without weight, we might say.

He does not feel, or see imaginatively, sympathetically, the advantages of habitual constancy. He feels only the truths of the other side, or the side of truth which he expresses when he says that all true passion is selfish; and passion and its truth are the final test for him. This selfishness, which is even more self-reliance than it is self-seeking, which has his instinctive approval in all moods, is directly celebrated by him in most. The more natural genius and originality one has, he says, the more one feels the profound truth of the remark of the Duchesse de Ferté, that she found no one but herself who was always right. And not only does natural genius, which we might sum up as honesty to one's instincts, or originality, make us contemptuous of all judgments but our own; it leads us (so far does Beyle go) to esteem only ourselves. Reason makes us see, and prevents our acting, since nothing is worth the effort it costs. Laziness forces us to prefer ourselves, and in others it is only ourselves that we esteem.

With this principle as his broadest generalization, it is not unnatural that his profoundest admiration was for Napoleon. I am a man, he says in substance, who has loved a few painters, a few people, and respected one man, — Napoleon. He respected a man who knew what he wanted, wanted it constantly, and pursued it fearlessly, without scruples and with intelligence, with constant calculation, with lies, with hypocrisy, with cruelty. Beyle used to lie with remarkable ease even in his youth. He makes his almost autobiographical hero, Julien Sorel, a liar throughout, and a hypocrite on the very day of his execution. Beyle lays down the judgments about Napoleon, — that he liked argument, because he was strong in it; and that he kept his peace, like a savage, whenever there was any possibility of his being seen to be inferior to any one else in grasp of the topic under discussion. It is in his "Life of Napoleon" that Beyle dwells as persistently as anywhere on his never-ceasing principle, — examine yourself; get at your most spontaneous, indubitable tastes, desires, ambitions; follow them; act from them unceasingly; be turned aside by nothing.

It is possible, in going through Beyle's works for that purpose, to find a remark here and there that might possibly indicate a basis of faith under this insistence, a belief that in the end a thorough independence of aim in each individual would be for the good of all; but these passing words really do not go against the truth of the statement that Beyle was absolutely without the moral attitude; that the pleasing to himself immediately was all he gave interest to, and that of the intellectual qualities those that had beauty for him were the crueller ones, — force, concentration, sagacity, in the service of egotism. But here are a few of the possible exceptions. "Molière," he says, in a dispute about that writer's morality, "painted with more depth than the other poets. Therefore he is more moral. Nothing could be more simple." With this epigram he leaves the subject; but it is tolerably clear that he means to deny any other moral than truth, not to say that the truth is an inevitable servant of good. If it did mean the latter, it was thrown off at the moment as an easy argument; for his belief is pronounced through his works, that his loves are the world's banes, and that any interest in the world's good, in the moral law, is *bourgeois* and dull. Here is another phrase that perhaps might suggest that the generalization was unsafe: "He is the greatest man in Europe because he is the only honest man." This, like the other, is clear enough to a reader of him; and it is really impossible to find in him any identification of the interesting, the worthy, with the permanently and generally serviceable. Where the social point of view is taken for a moment, it is by grace of logic purely, for a formal fairness. A more unmitigated moral rebel, a more absolute sceptic, a more thoroughly isolated individual than the author of "Le Rouge et le Noir" could not exist. Nor could a more unhesitating dogmatist exist, despite his sneering apologies; for dogmatism is as natural an expression of absolute scepticism as it is of absolute faith. When a man refuses to say anything further than, "This is true for me, at this moment," or perhaps, "This is true of a man exactly such as I describe, in exactly these circumstances," he is likely to make these statements with unshakable firmness. This distinctness and coherence of the mind which is entirely devoted to relativity, is one of the charms of Stendhal for his lovers. It makes possible the completeness and the originality of a perfect individual, of an entirely unrestrained growth. It is the kind of character that we call capricious or fantastic when it is weak; but when it is strong, it has a value for us through its emphasis of interesting principles which we do not find so visible and disentangled in more conforming people. The instincts which in Stendhal have such a free field to expatiate seem to some readers rare and distinguished, and to these readers it is a delight to see them set in such high relief. This, in its most general aspect, is what gave him his short-lived glory among the young writers of France. They hailed him as the discoverer of the doctrine of relativity, or as the first who applied it to the particular facts they wished to emphasize — the environment and its influence on the individual. This has been overworked by great men and little men until we grow sad at the sound of the word; but it was not so in Beyle's time, and he used the principle with moderation, seldom or never forgetting the incalculable and inexplicable accidents of individual variations. He does not forget either that individuals make the environment, and he is really clearer than his successors in treating race-traits, the climate and the local causes, individual training, and individual idiosyncrasies, as a great mixed whole, in which the safest course is to stick pretty closely to the study of the completed product. For this reason Zola very properly removed him from the pedestal on which Taine had put him, for what is a solvent of all problems to the school for which Taine hoped to be the prophet is in Stendhal but one principle, in its place on an equality with others. Zola's analysis of this side of Beyle is really masterly; and he proves without difficulty that the only connection between Beyle and the present naturalists is one of creed, not of execution — that Beyle did not apply the principle he believed in. The setting of his scenes is not distinct. Sometimes it is not even sketched in; and here Zola draws an illustration from a strong scene in "Le Rouge et le Noir," and shows how different the setting would have been in his own hands. Beyle is a logician, abstract; Zola thinks himself concrete, and concrete he is — often by main force. This is a sad failure to apply the doctrine of relativity to one's self. Beyle errs sometimes in the same way, and some of his attempts at local color are very tiresome, but on the whole he remains frankly the analyzer, the introspective psychologist, the man of distinct but disembodied ideas. He recognized the environment as he recognized other things in his fertile reflections, but he was, as a rule, too faithful to his own principles to spend much time in trying to reproduce it in details which did not directly interest him. It was therefore natural that his celebration by the extremists should be short-lived. Most of them do him what justice they can with effort, like Zola, or pass him over with some such word as the "dry" of Goncourt. His fads were his own. None of them have yet become the fads of a school, though some principles that were restrained with him have become battle-cries in later times. His real fads are hardly fitted to be banners, for they are too specific. In very general theories he generally kept rather sane. His real difference from the school that claimed him for a father half a century after his death, is well suggested in the awkward word that Zola is fond of throwing at him, "ideologist." The idea, the abstract truth and the intellectual form of it, its clearness, its statableness, its cogency and consistency, is the final interest with him. The outer world is only the material for the expression of ideas, only the illustrations of them, and the ideas are therefore not pictorial or dramatic, but logical. The arts are ultimately the expression of thought and feeling, and color and plastic form are means only. You never find him complaining, as his friend Mérimée did, that the meaning of the plastic arts cannot be given in words, because for a slight difference in shade or in curve there is no expression in language. All that Beyle got out of art he could put into words. He made no attempt to compete with the painter, like the leading realists of the past half-century. Other arts interested him only as far as they formed, without straining, illustrations for expression in language of the feelings they appeal to. It was with him in music as it was in painting, and often his musical criticism is as charming to the unattached *dilettante* as it is annoying to the technical critic who judges it in its own forms. Beyle names the sensation with precision always. His vocabulary has fine shades without weakening fluency. In choosing single words to name single sensations is his greatest power, and it is a power which naturally belongs to a man whose eye is inward, a power which the word-painters of the environment lack. Everything is expression for Beyle, and within the limits of the verbally-expressible he steadfastly remains. His truth is truth to the forms of thought as they exist in the reason — the clear eighteenth-century reason — disembodied truth.

> " It is necessary to have bones and blood in the human machine to make it walk. But we give slight attention to these necessary conditions of life, to fly to its great end, its final result — to think and to feel.
>
> " That is the history of drawing, of color, of light and shade, of all the various parts of painting, compared to expression.
>
> " Expression is the whole of art."

This reminds one again of Mérimée's statement, that Beyle could see in the Moses nothing but the expression of ferocity; and an equally conclusive assertion (for it is in him no confession) is made by Beyle in reference to music, which he says is excellent if it gives him elevated thoughts on the subjects that are occupying him, and if it makes him think of the music itself it is mediocre. Thus Beyle is as far from being an artist as possible. He cares for the forms of the outer world, he spends his life in looking at beauty and listening to it, but only because he knows that that is the way to call up in himself the ideas, the sensations, the emotions that he loves almost with voluptuousness. The basis of genius, he says, in speaking of Michelangelo, is logic, and if this is true — as in the sense in which he used it, it probably is — Beyle's genius was mostly basis.

Mérimée says that though Beyle was constantly appealing to logic, he reached his conclusions not by his reason but by his imagination. This is certainly making a false distinction. Beyle was not a logician in the sense that he got at conclusions indirectly by syllogisms. He did not forget his premises in the interest of the inductive process. What he calls logic is an attitude or quality of the mind, and means really abstract coherence. Of what he himself calls ideology, with as much contempt as Zola could put into the word, he says that it is a science not only tiresome but impertinent. He means any constructive, deductive system of thought. He studied Kant and other German metaphysicians, and thought them shallow — superior men ingeniously building houses of cards. His feet seldom if ever got off the solid ground of observations into the region of formal, logical deduction. "Facts! facts!" he cried, and his love of facts at first hand keeps him from some of the defects of the abstract mind. Every statement is independent of the preceding and the succeeding ones, each is examined by itself, each illustrated by anecdote, inexact enough, to be sure, but clear. There is no haze in his thought. When Mérimée says that it is Beyle's imagination and not his logic that decides, he is right, in the sense that Beyle has no middle terms, that his vision is direct, that the *a priori* process is secondary and merely suggestive with him. "What should we logically expect to find the case here?" he will ask before a new set of facts; but if his expectation and his observation differ, he readjusts his principles. It is no paradox to call a mind both abstract and empirical, introspective and scientific; and Beyle's was both.

This quality of logic without constructiveness shows, of course, in his style. There is lucidity of transition, of connection, of relation, among the details, but the parts are not put together to form an artistic whole. They fall on to the paper from his mind direct, and the completed book has no other unity than has the mind of the author. As he was a strong admirer of Bacon and his methods, it is safe enough to say that he would have accepted entirely this statement about composition as his own creed: —

"Thirdly, whereas I could have digested these rules into a certain method or order, which, I know, would have been more admired, as that which would have made every particular rule, through its coherence and relation unto other rules, seem more cunning and more deep; yet I have avoided so to do, because this delivering of knowledge in distinct and disjoined aphorisms doth leave the wit of man more free to turn and toss, and to make use of that which is so delivered to more several purposes and applications."

He is the typical suggestive critic, formless, uncreative, general and specific, precise and abstract: chaotic to the artist, satisfactory to the psychologist. It makes no difference where the story begins, whether this sentence follows that, or where the chapter ends. There are no rules of time and place. His style is a series of epigrams, and the order of their presentation is almost accidental. "To draw out a plot freezes me," he says, and one could guess it from his stories, which are in all essentials like his essays. To this analytic, unplastic mind the plot, the characters, are but illustrations of the general truths. The characters he draws have separate individual life only so far as they are copies. There is no invention, no construction, no creation. Moreover, there is no style, or no other quality of style than lucidity. He not only lacks other qualities, he despises them. The "neatly turned" style and the rhetorical alike have his contempt. Most rhetoricians are "emphatic, eloquent, and declamatory." He almost had a duel about Chateaubriand's "cime indéterminée des forêts." Rousseau is particularly irritating to him. "Only a great soul knows how to write simply, and that is why Rousseau has put so much rhetoric into the 'New Eloïse,' which makes it unreadable after thirty years." In another place he says he detests, in the arrangement of words, tragic combinations, which are intended to give majesty to the style. He sees only absurdity in them. His style fits his thought, and his failure to comprehend color in style is not surprising in a man whose thought has no setting, in a man who remarks with scorn that it is easier to describe clothing than it is to describe movements of the soul. He cares only for movements of the soul. The sense of form might have given his work a larger life, but it is part of his rare value for a few that he talks in bald statements, single-word suggestions, disconnected flashes. This intellectual impressionism, as it were, is more stimulating to them than any work of art. These are not poetic souls, it is needless to say, however much they may love poetry. Beyle is the essence of prose, and it is his strength. He loved poetry, but he got from it only the prose, so much of the idea as is independent of the form. Mérimée tells us that Beyle murdered verse in reading aloud, and in his treatise "De l'Amour" Beyle informs us that verse was invented to help the memory, and to retain it in dramatic art is a remnant of barbarity. The elevation, the *abandon*, the passion of poetry — all but the psychology — were foreign to this mind, whose unimaginative prose is its distinction.

Perhaps this limitation is kin to another: that as novelist Beyle painted with success only himself. Much the solidest of his characters is Julien Sorel, a copy trait for trait of the author, reduced, so to speak, to his essential elements. Both Julien and Beyle were men of restless ambition, clear, colorless minds, and constant activity. Julien turned this activity to one thing, the study of the art of dominating women, and Beyle to three, of which this was the principal, and the other two were the comprehension of art principles and the expression of them. In his earlier days he had followed the army of Napoleon, until he became disgusted with the grossness of the life he saw. What renown he won in the army was for making his toilet with complete care on the eve of battle. From the Moscow army he wrote to one of his friends that everything was lacking which he needed, — "friendship, love (or the semblance of it), and the arts." For simplicity, friendship may be left out in summing up Beyle's interests, for while his friendships were genuine they did not interest him much, except as an opportunity to work up his ideas. Of the two interests that remain, the one expressed in Julien, the psychology of love, illustrated by practice, is much the more essential. Julien too had Napoleon for an ideal, and when he found he could not imitate him in the letter he resigned himself to making in his spirit the conquests that were open to him. The genius that Napoleon put into political relations he would put into social ones. All the principles of war should live again in his intrigues with women.

This spirit is well enough known in its outlines. Perhaps the most perfect sketch of it in its unmixed form is in "Les Liaisons Dangereuses," a book which Beyle knew and must have loved. He must have admired and envied the Comte de Valmont and the Marquise de Merteuil. There is here none of the grossness of the Restoration comedy in England. It is the art of satisfying vanity in a particular way, in its most delicate form. It is an occupation and an art as imperative, one might almost say as impersonal, were not the paradox so violent, as any other. What makes Stendhal's account of this art differ from that of Delaclos and the other masters is the fact that, deeply as he is in it, he is half outside of it: he is the psychologist every moment, seeing his own attitude as coldly as he sees the facts on which he is forming his campaign. Read the scene, for instance, where Julien first takes the hand of the object of his designs, absolutely as a matter of duty, a disagreeable move necessary to the success of the game. The cold, forced spirit of so much of intrigue is clearly seen by Beyle and accepted by him as a necessity. He used to tell young men that if they were alone in a room five minutes with a beautiful woman without declaring they loved her, it proved them poltroons. Two sides of him, however, are always present; for this is the same man who repeats forever in his book the cry that there is no love in France. He means that this science, better than no love at all, is inferior to the *abandon* of the Italians. The love of 1770, for which he often longs, with its gayety, its tact, its discretion "with the thousand qualities of *savoir-vivre*," is after all only second. *Amour-gout*, to point out the distinction in two famous phrases of his own, is forever inferior to *amour-passion*. Stendhal, admiring the latter, must have been confined to the former, though not in its baldest form, for to some of the skill and irony of Valmont he added the softness, the sensibility, of a later generation, and he added also the will to feel, so that his study of feeling and his practice of it grew more successful together. Psychology and sensibility are mutual aids in him, as they not infrequently are in "observers of the human heart," to quote his description of his profession. "What consideration can take precedence, in a sombre heart, of the never-flagging charm of being loved by a woman who is happy and gay?" The voluptuary almost succeeds in looking as genuine as the psychologist. "This nervous fluid, so to speak, has each day but a certain amount of sensitiveness to expend. If you put it into the enjoyment of thirty beautiful pictures you shall not use it to mourn the death of an adored mistress." You cannot disentangle them. Love, voluptuousness, art, psychology, sincerity, effort, all are mixed up together, whatever the ostensible subject. It is a truly French compound, perhaps made none the less essentially French by the author's constant berating of his country for its consciousness and vanity: a man who would be uneasy if he were not exercising his fascinating powers on some woman, and a man whose tears were ready; a man who could not live without action, soaking in the *dolce far niente;* a man all intelligence, and by very force of intelligence a man of emotion. He would be miserable if he gave himself up to either side. "In the things of sentiment perhaps the most delicate judges are found at Paris — but there is always a little chill." He goes to Italy; and as he voluptuously feels the warm air and sees the warm blood and the free movements, the simplicity of heedlessness and passion, his mind goes back longingly to the other things.

"All is decadence here, all in memory. Active life is in London and in Paris. The days when I am all sympathy I prefer Rome; but staying here tends to weaken the mind, to plunge it into stupor. There is no effort, no energy, nothing moves fast. Upon my word, I prefer the active life of the North and the bad taste of our barracks."

But among these conflicting ideals it is possible perhaps to pick the strongest, and I think it is painted in this picture: "A delicious salon, within ten steps of the sea, from which we are separated by a grove of orange-trees. The sea breaks gently, Ischia is in sight. The ices are excellent." The last touch is all Beyle. What is more subtle to a man whose whole life is an experiment in taste, what more suggestive, what more typical, than an ice? There is a pervading delight in it, in the unsubstantiality, the provokingness, the refinement of it. "In the boxes, toward the middle of the evening, the *cavaliere servante* of the lady usually orders some ices. There is always some wager, and the ordinary bets are sherbets, which are divine. There are three kinds, *gelati*, *crepè*, and *pezzidiere.* It is an excellent thing to become familiar with. I have not yet determined the best kind, and I experiment every evening." Do not mistake this for playfulness. The man who cannot take an ice seriously cannot take Stendhal sympathetically.

Such, in the rough, is the point of view of this critic of character and of art. Of course the value of judgments from such a man in such an attitude is dependent entirely on what one seeks from criticism. Here is what Stendhal hopes to give:—

> "My end is to make each observer question his own soul, disentangle his own manner of feeling, and thus succeed in forming a judgment for himself, a way of seeing formed in accord with his own character, his tastes, his ruling passions, if indeed he have passions, for unhappily they are necessary to judge the arts."

The word "passion," here as elsewhere, is not to be given too violent a meaning. "Emotion" would do as well — sincere personal feeling. That there is no end of art except to bring out this sincere individual feeling is his ultimate belief. He is fond of the story of the young girl who asked Voltaire to hear her recite, so as to judge of her fitness for the stage. Astonished at her coldness, Voltaire said: "But, mademoiselle, if you yourself had a lover who abandoned you, what would you do?" "I would take another," she answered. That, Stendhal adds, is the correct point of view for nineteen-twentieths of life, but not for art. "I care only for genius, for young painters with fire in the soul and open intelligence." For disinterested, cool taste, for objective justness and precision, he has only contempt. Indeed, he accepts Goethe's definition of taste as the art of properly tying one's cravats in things of the mind. Everything that is not special to the speaker, personal, he identifies with thinness, insincerity, pose. "The best thing one can bring before works of art, is a natural mind. One must dare to feel what he does feel." To be one's self, the first of rules, means to follow one's primitive sentiments. "Instead of wishing to judge according to literary principles, and defend correct doctrines, why do not our youths content themselves with the fairest privilege of their age, to have sentiments?" There is no division into impersonal judgment and private sentiment. The only criticism that has value is private, personal, intimate.

Less special to Stendhal now, though rare at the time in which he lived, is the appeal to life as the basis of art. "To find the Greeks, look in the forests of America." Go to the swimming-school or the ballet to realize the correctness and the energy of Michelangelo. Familiarity is everything.

"The work of genius is the sense of conversation," and as "the man who takes the word of another is a cruel bore in a salon," so is he as a critic. "What is the antique bas-relief to me? Let us try to make good modern painting. The Greeks loved the nude. We never see it, and moreover it repels us." This conclusion shows the weakness, or the limitation, of this kind of criticism, which as Stendhal applies it would keep us from all we have learned from the revived study of the nude, because the first impression to one unused to seeing it is not an artistic one. But the limitations of Stendhal and his world are obvious enough. It is his eloquence and usefulness within his limits that are worth examination.

"Beauty," to Stendhal, "is simply a promise of happiness," and the phrase sums up his attitude. Here is his ideal way of taking music. He asked a question of a young woman about somebody in the audience. The young woman usually says nothing during the evening. To his question she answered, "Music pleases when it puts your soul in the evening in the same position that love put it in during the day."

Beyle adds: "Such is the simplicity of language and of action. I did not answer, and I left her. When one feels music in such a way, what friend is not importunate?" When he leaves this field for technical judgments, he is laughable to any one who does not care for the texture of his mind, whatever his expression; for music to him is really only a background for his sensibility. "How can I talk of music without giving the history of my sensations?" This is, doubtless, maudlin to the sturdy masculine mind, this religion of sensibility, this fondling of one's sentimental susceptibilities, and it certainly has no grandeur and no morality.

"Sensibility," Coleridge says, "that is, a constitutional quickness of sympathy with pain and pleasure, and a keen sense of the gratifications that accompany social intercourse, mutual endearments, and reciprocal preferences . . . sensibility is not even a sure pledge of a good heart, though among the most common meanings of that many-meaning and too commonly misapplied expression."

It leads, he goes on, to effeminate sensitiveness by making us alive to trifling misfortunes. This is just, with all its severity, and the lover of Stendhal has only to smile, and quote Rousseau, with Beyle himself: "I must admit that I am a great booby; for I get all my pleasure in being sad."

Naturally enough, *ennui* plays a great part in such a nature, thin, intelligent, sensitive, immoral, self-indulgent. It lies behind his art of love and his love of art. "*Ennui*, this great motive power of intelligent people," he says; and again: "I was much surprised when, studying painting out of pure *ennui*, I found it a balm for cruel sorrows." He really loves it. "*Ennui!* the god whom I implore, the powerful god who reigns in the hall of the *Français*, the only power in the world that can cause the Laharpes to be thrown into the fire." Hence his love for Madame du Deffand, the great expert in *ennui*, and for the whole century of *ennui*, wit, and immorality. Certainly the lack of all fire and enthusiasm, the lack of faith, of hope, of charity, does go often with a clear, sharp, negative freshness of judgment, which is often seen in the colder, finer, smaller workmen in the psychology of social relations. It is a great exposer of pretence. It enables Stendhal to see that most honest Northerners say in their hearts before the statues of Michelangelo, "Is that all?" as they say before their accomplished ideal, "Good Lord! to be happy, to be loved, is it only this?"

But just as Stendhal keeps in the borderland between vice and virtue, shrinking from grossness, and laughing at morality, so he cannot really cross into the deepest unhappiness any more than he could into passionate happiness. Tragedy repelled him. "The fine arts ought never to try to paint the inevitable ills of humanity. They only increase them, which is a sad success. . . . Noble and almost consoled grief is the only kind that art should seek to produce." To these half-tones his range is limited through the whole of his being. Of his taste in architecture, of which he was technically as ignorant as he was of music, Mérimée tells us that he disliked Gothic, thinking it ugly and sad, and liked the architecture of the Renaissance for its elegance and coquetry; that it was always graceful details, moreover, and not the general plan that attracted him; which is a limitation that naturally goes with the other.

Of course the charm and the short-comings that are everywhere in Beyle's art criticism are the same in his judgments of national traits, which form a large part of his work. Antipathy to the French is one of his fixed ideas, thorough Frenchman that he was; for his own vanity and distrust did not make him hate the less genuinely those weaknesses. Vanity is *bourgeois*, he thinks, and there is for him no more terrible word. It spoils the best things, too — conversation among others; for the French conversation is work.

"The most tiresome defect in our present civilization is the desire to produce effect." So with their bravery, their love, all is calculated, there is no abandonment. This annoys him particularly in the women, who are always the most important element to him. He gives them their due, but coldly: "France, however, is always the country where there are always the most passable women. They seduce by delicate pleasures made possible by their mode of dress, and these pleasures can be appreciated by the most passionless natures. Dry natures are afraid of Italian beauty." Of course this continual flinging at the French is only partly vanity, self-glorification in being able, almost alone of foreigners, to appreciate the Italians. It is partly contempt for his leading power, for mere intelligence. In his youth he spoke with half-regret of his being so reasonable that he would go to bed to save his health even when his head was crowded with ideas that he wanted to write. It was his desperate desire to be as

Italian as he could, rather than any serene belief that he had thrown off much of his French nature, that made him leave orders to have inscribed on his tombstone:—

Qui Giace
Arrigo Beyle Milanese
Visse, scrisse, amò.

It comes dangerously near to a pose, perhaps, and yet there is genuineness enough in it to make it pathetic. He praises the Italians because they do not judge their happiness. He never ceased to judge his. Nowhere outside of Italy, he thinks, can one hear with a certain accent, "O Dio! com' e bello!" But the implication is quite unfair. I have heard a common Frenchwoman exclaim, under her breath, before an ugly peacock, "Dieu! comme c'est beau," with an intensity that was not less because it was restrained. But restraint was Beyle's bugbear. From his own economical, calculating nature he flew almost with worship to its opposite. He is speaking of Julien and therefore of himself, when he says, in "Le Rouge et le Noir:" "Intellectual love has doubtless more cleverness than true love, but it has only moments of enthusiasm. It knows itself too well. It judges itself unceasingly. Far from driving away thought, it exists only by force of thought." He calls Julien mediocre, and he says of him, "This dry soul felt all of passion that is possible in a person raised in the midst of this excessive civilization which Paris admires." Beyle saves Julien from contempt at the end (and doubtless he consoled himself with something similar) by causing him, while remaining a conscious hypocrite, to lose his life unhesitatingly, absurdly, perversely, for the sake of love. Once he has shown himself capable of the divine unreason, of exaltation, he is respectable. Where the enthusiasm is he is blinded; he cannot see the crudity and stupidity of passion. Before this mad enthusiasm the French fineness and proportion is insignificant. He loses his memory of the charm he has told so well. "Elsewhere there is no conception of this art of giving birth to the laugh of the mind, and of giving delicious joys by unexpected words."

As might be expected, Beyle is even more unfair to the Germans than he is to his countrymen; for the sentiment of which he is the epicure and the apologist, has nothing in common with the reverent and poetic sentiment in which the Germans are so rich.

This last Beyle hates as he hates Rousseau and Madame de Staël. It is phrase, moonshine, and the fact that it is bound up in a stable and orderly character but makes it the more irritating. They are sentimental, innocent, and unintelligent, he says, and he quotes with a sneer, as true of the race, "A soul honest, sweet, and peaceful, free of pride and remorse, full of benevolence and humanity, above the nerves and the passions." In short, quite anti-Beylian, quite submissive, sweet, and moral. For England he has much more respect, and even a slight affection. He likes their anti-classicism, and he likes especially the beauty of their women, which he thinks second only to that of the Italians. The rich complexions, the free, open countenances, the strong forms rouse him sometimes almost to enthusiasm; but of course it is all secondary in the inevitable comparison. "English beauty seems paltry, without soul, without life, before the divine eyes which heaven has given to Italy." The somewhat in the submissive faces of the Englishwomen that threatens future *ennui*, Stendhal thinks has been ingrained there by the workings of the terrible law of propriety which rules as a despot over the unfortunate island. It is the vision of caprice in the face of the Italian woman that makes him certain of never being bored.

It is not surprising that women should be the objects through which Beyle sees everything. A man who sees in relativity, arbitrariness, caprice, the final law of nature, and who feels a sympathy with this law, not unnaturally finds in the absolute, personal, perverse nature of women his most congenial companionship. He finds in women something more elemental than reasonableness. He finds the basal instincts. They best illustrate his psychology of final, absolute choice. Of course there is the other side too, the epicure's point of view, from which their charm is the centre of the paradise of leisure, music, and ices. His hyperbole in praising art is "equal to the first handshake of the woman one loves." In politics he sees largely the relations of sex; and in national character it is almost always of the women he is talking. Their influence marks the advance of civilization. "Tenderness has made progress among us because society has become more perfect," and tenderness here is this soft or, if you choose, effeminate, sensibility.

"The admission of women to perfect equality would be the surest sign of civilization. It would double the intellectual forces of the human race and its probabilities of happiness. . . . To attain equality, the source of happiness for both sexes, the duel would have to be open to women; the pistol demands only address. Any woman, by subjecting herself to imprisonment for two years, would be able, at the expiration of the term, to get a divorce. Towards the year Two Thousand these ideas will be no longer ridiculous."

In this passage is the whole man, intelligent and fantastic, sincere and suspicious, fresh, convincing, absurd. He is rapidly settling back into obscurity, to which he is condemned as much by the substance of his thought as by the formlessness of its expression. Entirely a rebel, and only slightly a revolutionist, he is treated by the world as he treated it. A lover of many interesting things inextricably wound up together, his earnest talk about them will perhaps for some time longer be an important influence on the lives of a few whose minds shall be of the kind to which a sharp, industrious, capricious, and rebellious individual is the best stimulant to their own thought.

1894.

MÉRIMÉE AS A CRITIC

V

MÉRIMÉE AS A CRITIC

Prosper Mérimée, perhaps the most skilful of French short story-tellers, has talked of his art preferences in essays little inferior in execution to his tales, and revealed in them the most attractive side of his own nature, and yet most of them lie hidden in the files of "Le Constitutionel," "Le Temps," "Les Débats," and "La Revue des Deux Mondes." Indeed, the powers which charm the lover of deftness in literature sometimes appear even more distinctly when he is speaking his critical opinion than they do when he is telling a story. For this reason the essays are almost unique in form. It would be hard to find another example of an art of this kind, — the kind that has gone into the best short fiction, the art in which the execution is the most prominent merit, the perfectly chiselled miniature, shown in miscellaneous critical essays. Why, then, does no one study his criticism?

We know his irony in his stories. When, after the death of Carmen, the reader comes suddenly to a comment on certain gypsy words, he feels it. He feels it at the death of Arsène, surrounded by the doctor, her lover, and the great lady who with her piety has deprived the dying peasant of her lover, and is herself in danger of falling, with all her virtue, a prey to the same man. He feels it as, after this scene, he reads this last chapter; with the epitaph written by the woman of prayer over the grave of the girl who had known only one love, and had had that taken from her as immoral by the virtuous woman who appropriated it.

"Well, madam, you tell me that my story is finished and that you do not care to hear more. I should think you would be curious to know whether or not M. de Salligny made his trip to Greece; whether — but it is late, and you have had enough. So be it. At least avoid hasty judgments, for I protest that I have said nothing to authorize them. Especially, do not doubt the truth of my story. Are you sceptical? Go to Père Lachaise; twenty feet to the left of the tomb of General Foy, you will find a very simple lias stone, surrounded by flowers that are always well tended. On the stone you can read the name of my heroine cut in large letters: ARSÈNE GUILLOT. And if you bend over this tomb you will see, if the rain has not already erased it, a line written with a lead-pencil, in a very fine hand:

"'Poor Arsène! She is praying for us.'"

The charm of the irony is, like the charm of the execution, in distance, in delicacy of suggestion. In his essays, this preference for less obvious methods of suggestion, the dislike of the easy and the explicit, is stated. "He found her *piquante*, to use one of those expressions that I hate." And in his essay on Nicholas Gogol he wrote a passage that is at once a good illustration of his essay style, and an open expression of his impatience with commonplace methods in literature:—

"I think the study well done and graphically depicted, as M. Diaforus would say, but I don't like the kind; madness is one of the misfortunes which move us, but also disgust. Doubtless by putting a madman into his story a writer is sure of making an effect. He moves a cord always sensitive, but the means is vulgar, and the talent of M. Gogol is not one of those that need to descend to these trivialities. Let us leave madmen to beginners, with the dogs, those characters of an equally irresistible effect. What a glory to wring tears from your reader if you break a poodle's leg! Homer, in my opinion, is excusable for making us weep at the mutual recognition of the dog Argus and Ulysses only because he was, I believe, the first to discover the resources offered by the canine race to an author at the end of expedients."

Thus the essays have the same severity that distinguishes the art of his stories. More important, however, to the student of Mérimée is the fact that they give another side of him, — a side that a careful reader might guess from the stories, a side that is more openly suggested in his letters, but which even in the letters shows itself only timidly and indirectly. It is a rather singular fact that straightforward seriousness should show itself clearly in the essays alone. In them he tells without sarcasm the principles of art in which he believes. He describes the art that charms him and moves him. He talks of friendship, too, in a tone that he would shrink from using in a letter. It seems as if he knew the public expected this, and would not laugh at him for it as a friend might. The Mérimée of the letters and stories is an artist of brilliancy, force, and elegance, but a man who is always on the defensive, protecting himself from ridicule by distance. Timidity or taste makes him avoid always a serious tone. The Mérimée of the essays is the skilful artist still, and he is besides a man of broad comprehension and sympathy. It would be hard to find in his letters or stories as simple a tone as the one in these words about a story of Gogol's:

> "I hasten to come to a little masterpiece, 'An Oldtime Household.' In a few pages M. Gogol tells us the lives of two good old people, husband and wife, living in the country, persons in whose heads there is no grain of malice, deceived and adored by their peasants, ingeniously egotistic because they believe all the world happy, as they are themselves. The wife dies. The husband, who had seemed to live only to eat, fails and dies a few months after his wife. We laugh and cry in reading this charming tale, where the art of the story-teller is hidden in the simplicity of the story. All is true, natural. There is no detail which is not charming and a part of the general effect."

In personal affection it is the same. He shrank from speaking seriously of affection, orally or in letters, and yet there is in his essay on Victor Jacquemont sincere feeling, entirely undisguised and unclothed in irony. He dwells with fondness over some of the various traits of the character, and when he comes to speak of his voice, he uses a quotation singularly warm for him: "When I heard him speak I used to think of these lines of Shakespeare:—

"'Oh! it came on my ears like the sweet South
That breathes upon a bank of violets.'"

An essay that shows strong literary affection is one on Madame du Deffand in "Le Moniteur" for April 29, 1867. Nobody has entered with more accurate sympathy into the character of the famous wit. Mérimée speaks simply a real love of the woman and of the period. He does not garble the facts, but he is lenient because he feels the eloquence of Madame du Deffand from her own point of view; he feels her loyalty to her first impressions, her frankness, her desire to please, the simplicity and elevation of her intellectual tastes. He felt, too, the genuineness of her ephemeral affections, and he knew the sincerity in the seeming frivolity. It is a passing book review, and yet it shows better than anything else he has written his appreciation of one kind of mind.

Simple liking for certain things and certain people is not the only trait of character which is seen clearly only in the essays. Another trait, allied to it, is intellectual charity. In his letters, Mérimée's criticisms of things he does not like are sharp and contemptuous. That he could speak with more reserve in his rôle of a professional critic is shown in an essay on the English pre-Raphaelite art in "La Revue des Deux Mondes" for October 15, 1857. Nothing could be further from his sympathy; nothing could be in sharper contrast with his skill in economy and convergence of parts than their pointless details; nothing more different from his restraint and fineness than their efforts for literary symbolism. Of course he saw their weaknesses, but he also saw their merits. The weaknesses are described, for him, with little bitterness or sarcasm. Here is a description of a picture by Hunt:—

"A young woman is singing before an open piano. She holds in her hand a sheet of music. Behind her is a young man in morning dress, with his arm passed gayly about her waist. Her mouth is open; probably she is running a division; but she has a frightful grimace, and, moreover, as I learned by putting on my spectacles, she has tears in her eyes. Beside this group, in an easy-chair, is a cat which shares the taste of Harlequin, of whom it is well known that he liked only those serenades at which there is food. This cat has procured for itself a canary, and is in the process of killing it.

. . . I wished to know why this fair singer wept, while her companion was so gay. Unfortunately the title was very laconic, 'Conscience Awakened.' I admit that I was more puzzled than I had been before I had resorted to the catalogue. Fortunately I met an English artist, who gave me the following explanation: 'You certainly see that the two persons in this picture are not demeaning themselves properly. Look at the hand of the young woman. . . You will notice that she has no marriage ring, and is therefore unmarried. The arm passed about her waist shows that she has a lover. She is singing one of Moore's melodies, which you ought to know by heart, and of which you can easily read the title by standing on your head. This title will remind you that in the third couplet the unfortunate woman meets an allusion to her own false position, and this allusion chokes her in the midst of the *roulade*. It is then that her conscience is awakened, and there you have what Mr. Hunt has expressed.' 'And the cat?' I asked. 'The cat is at once an interesting detail and a moral. It represents the bad instincts, and the canary represents innocence, two well-chosen emblems.'"

Yet even in a school so ridiculous to him Mérimée finds good, and points out the various technical merits with fairness. Even in Mr. Ruskin he sees a use. He says Mr. Ruskin has a few ideas that are sane, even practicable, and that these ideas have been made more effective in England by the violence of their expression. His general impression of the pre-Raphaelites is thus put: "Habits of reflection, a taste for subtlety, pretension to depth, mixed with a great deal of inexperience," and, he adds later, an entire lack of comprehension of the noble style.

His technique in the essays is worth as much study by young critics as young novelists put on his stories. It is almost impossible to see the logic of the arrangement, and quite impossible not to feel that there is logic. Though there is no apparent synthesis, the man of whom he writes stands out; the picture is finished, given in a few strokes. He is abrupt, but not incomplete. His bold unity is beyond analysis. There are few introductions, no conclusions, and no obvious ornament. His dislike of the opposite method of express transition and setting he has suggested in "Charles IX." in an imaginary dialogue between the reader and the author:—

"Ah, Mr. Author, what a fine chance you have here to draw portraits! And such portraits! You will take us to the castle at Madrid, in the midst of the court — and such a court! Are you going to show it to us, this French-Italian court? Introduce us in turn to all the distinguished characters. How much we shall learn, and how interesting will be the day spent among such grand persons!

"Alas, Mr. Reader, what a request you are making! I would fain have the talent to write a history of France; I should not then be telling stories. But tell me, why do you wish me to introduce to you persons who play no part in my novel?

"You do a great wrong in not giving them parts in it. What, you take me back to the year 1572, and then pretend to escape the portrayal of so many remarkable men! Come, you cannot hesitate. Begin, and I shall give you the first phrase: *The door of the salon opened, and there appeared* . . .

"But, Mr. Reader, there were no salons in the castle of Madrid. Salons . . .

"Well. *The great hall was filled with a crowd,* . . . etc. . . . *among whom might be distinguished* . . . etc.

"What do you wish to have distinguished?

"Of course, in the first place, Charles IX! . . .

"And in the second?

"Not so fast. First you must describe his costume, then you will give a portrait of his appearance, and finally of his character. That is to-day the high road for all novelists.

"His costume? He was in hunting dress, with a great huntsman's horn about his neck.

"You are short . . ."

Mérimée then yields and gives a sketch in his own manner: —

"Well, imagine a young man rather well formed, with his head a little sunk into his shoulders, his neck stretched out, and his face thrown awkwardly forward. His nose is rather large, the lips are fine and long, the upper one protruding. His complexion is wan, and his large green eyes never look at the person to whom he is talking. Moreover, it is impossible to read in his eyes *Saint Bartholomew*, or anything like it. No, his expression is rather stupid and restless than hard or savage."

In the historical essays Mérimée's art does not work as well as in the literary essays.

"I like in history only anecdotes, and among the anecdotes I prefer those in which I think I see a true picture of the customs and characteristics of the epoch. This is not a noble taste, but I admit to my shame that I would freely give up Thucydides for some authentic memoirs of Aspasia or of one of the slaves of Pericles; for memoirs, which are familiar talks of the author with the reader, alone furnish those portraits of man which amuse and interest me."

As an example, he quotes this "concise note" from "L'Étoile": —

"The young lady of Châteauneuf, one of the favorites of the king before he went to Poland, having made a love marriage with Antinotti, a Florentine, an overseer of galley slaves at Marseilles, and having found him wantoning, killed him like a man with her own hands. . . . Out of this story and the many others of which Brantôme is full my imagination builds a character, and I call to life a woman of the court of Henry the Third."

This taste makes Mérimée a success as a writer of historical essays only where the subject is fitted to concise narrative, where the bearing is apparent without explanation. In some essays, "Les Cosaques d'Autrefois and les Faux Demetrius," for instance, he is hard to read, for the stories are long and not interesting in outline, and the dulness of them is only emphasized by Mérimée's bareness of statement. One feels as Mérimée himself felt of Sallust: —

"In a long work his style might weary, on account of a conciseness which is perhaps not sufficiently free from mannerism. Applied to short tales it produces the deepest impression, by combining energy of thought with sobriety of setting. Art sometimes shows itself in this style a little too openly, in spite of the affectation of disorder in the composition, and one frequently forgets the interest of the story to admire the skill of the story-teller."

The opinions expressed in the essays make us like Mérimée far more than do the truculent condemnations of the letters. Sometimes, of course, he is unsympathetic, but seldom or never caustic.

"Michelangelo," he says, "has conceived his Moses as an athlete. I will be bold enough to say that this savage giant, with arms like a porter's and a beard of ropes, does not to me represent the guide and prophet of the Hebrews. He is a man whom no one would care to meet in the woods, but who would not know how to force obedience from a stiff-necked race."

He does not like what he thinks the exaggerated grandeur that Plutarch and Shakespeare give to Cæsar, but he likes still less the method of Suetonius.

"Very different from Plutarch, who gives all his heroes the grand air, Suetonius seems to have delighted in belittling his. His is a low and spiteful mind that cannot understand genius. He has neither indignation for vice nor enthusiasm for virtue, but he seeks everywhere ridicule, because ridicule levels all reputations and destroys both terror and admiration. Suetonius shows his whole nature in his life of Cæsar. He gives but a few pages to his many remarkable deeds, but he finds space to repeat in full the devilish songs of the soldiers who accompanied in his triumph the conqueror of the world."

This last quotation has the tone that can seldom be found in any of Mérimée's work but his essays. Apparently he enjoyed them less than his stories and his letters, so it may be that the tone of seriousness, here even severe, is one that represents him less intimately than his pervading irony. Yet his character is the broader, that he could speak in that tone so well. And it is not at all certain, merely because he was usually half contemptuous in his art and in his personal relations, that he did not have as genuinely the gentler and simpler emotions and preferences that can be seen in his criticism. It is not unlikely that his own words about Beyle apply to himself: —

". . . the fear of being through a dupe, and the constant care to avoid this misfortune ; hence this factitious hardening, this despairing analysis of low motives in all generous action, this resistance to the first impulses of the heart, much more affected than real with him, it seems to me."

Certainly this timid narrowing is, whatever the cause, much less constant in his essays. Therefore, to read Mérimée's criticism after knowing his letters and stories, is to see an expression of the more generous side of him. It is to be able, in judging him, to see him less limited to irony, to see him as a man of wider range.

1895.

AMERICAN ART CRITICISM

VI

AMERICAN ART CRITICISM

I

In contrast to the common assertion that the American race is developing in its feelings for life and expression some traits prominent in the French is the fact that in our contemporary literature we are almost weakest where the French are strongest. We who in the arts which are less generally followed here, in painting and sculpture, have contributed to the first rank of artists, and are respectable at least in fiction, are in an art which is much more practised here, that of criticism, really insignificant. Although in no country do people read more, in no country of importance is the current comment on books more lacking in thought and workmanship. In short stories we are doing something firm and individual, but in the art of which in a nation of readers we might expect high development, we are to-day as far behind France and even England as we are in poetry. In comment on the drama, the same low level is unbroken. Although we are a theatre-going nation we have nobody with the knowledge of the stage which makes experts of Sarcey, Archer, and Lemaitre; nobody with the literary charm put into dramatic criticism of Walkley or Anatole France. Strangely enough, the most interesting criticism of the day is put upon those arts of which our people know least. Are there many present commentators on books in the United States who have the subtlety, the fine edge, the intellectual fineness shown in Mr. Brownell's criticism of art? Is there to be found in much of our literary criticism the grave certainty and elevation of Mr. La Farge, or the results of study, contact, energy, and high aim which meet in the style of Mrs. Van Rensselaer and make it alive even when it is rough? These critics in their speech sound important, they have the undertone of feeling and understanding, they stand for grasp and choice. How often can they be matched among the living American writers whose volumes deal with books? To add one other to the list, who of our literary critics gives the clear, informal explanations of technical faults and successes that are thrown off in anonymous judgments of contemporary pictures and books on painting by the strict and lawyerlike pen of Mr. Cox?

The explanation of these seemingly anomalous conditions is to be found in what at first sight appears to constitute the anomalies. It is the size of our reading public that keeps our literary criticism lower than our creative work in literature and the plastic arts and lower than our art criticism. We read not only more books than the people of other countries, but more newspapers also; and it is the newspaper which partly sets and entirely represents average American standards. The large amount of space given in the dailies to literature and drama forms a contrast to the quality of the treatment. They must give the crowd what it will take immediately. They, the newspapers, aiming at great circulations; the plays, aiming at popular runs; the books, aiming at immediate sale, are all largely formed by the taste of that part of humanity which in other countries, where there is no popular education, has little to do with literature. Small and few indeed among us are the sets yet formed which raise and nourish men who care more for the mild approval of the judicious than for the money and the notoriety of popular success. Suppose that an American understood the mechanism of the drama as well as M. Sarcey, say, or Mr. Archer, would he be found out and encouraged by our journals? For a critic as erudite as M. Brunetière what respect, what dignity is there here compared to what France offers to solid work? What newspaper in America would not call an unknown Walkley or Anatole France "too literary"? How many editors frankly tell contributors that literary excellence is nothing; that popularity of subject is everything! Thus it is that the size of the audience which listens to the critic here makes him speak like a stump-orator. The very possibilities of criticism keep from it healthy encouragement. The crowd will not be led too fast. We support literary criticism in but one weekly of the same class with the French and English, and in but one daily. Expert handling of what we all feel capable of handling bores us, and even insults us. There is a story, probably true, that the owner of a great New York paper discharged his dramatic editor and openly announced his preference for ordinary reporters as critics of the theatre; and book-reviews in that as in most of our publications are the side issues of untrained men. The principal exception consists of the careless opinions of men who are famous for other things, and these opinions, being bought for the signature, are almost always miserable. How many readers know of the existence of Mr. Brownell compared to the number who read the trivialities published by prominent novelists whose critical faculties are so feeble that they are rightly treated with condescension by even the newspapers? When one of these prominent men does write criticisms he is careful not to go over the heads of his readers or to hurt the man who says, as so many say, "Perhaps I don't know what is good, but I know what I like," meaning that his opinion is as good as another's. The action of the committee of the Army of the Tennessee, overruling as unintelligent the decision of the Sculptors' Society, to which they had submitted designs for a statue of Sherman, is fresh in our minds. We will accept facts from experts, but our opinions are our own.

It is his own opinion, therefore, that the average reader has reflected back to him by the newspapers and magazines. One characteristic of his opinion is that it is not artistic but ethical. For instance, we do not find expositions of the methods of Ibsen, Pinero, or Dumas, to take three men remarkable for technical qualities, but homilies on the character of Mrs. Tanqueray or on the fitness of showing "certain things" to the public. Instead of enthusiasm like that of the elder Dumas over his son's skill in getting his heroine back to Paris after the third act of La Dame aux Camelias, we have soliloquies on the possibility of Marguerite's being so refined in her occupation. Of the few dailies most read by cultivated Americans, two have for dramatic critics men whose moral tone is so high that they are actually unacquainted with the unwholesome plays of France; and I have seen a musical critic of prominence leave the opera-house after the first act at the first presentation of "Manon," because it followed the novel too closely, to write the next day a scathing dismissal of the opera. Nowhere do we get the detachment, penetration, and learning that must combine to make an equipped critic of books or plays. The only one among those New York papers worthy of notice which is free from Jeromiac concern lacks artistic seriousness, too, and aims only at jocosity. Our critics do not study foreign models, they do not study their subjects, and they do not have the general attitude of culture which is more needed by the critic than by any other artist. Without these difficult acquirements they can, with instincts compounded of ethical obsessions and carelessness of art, mirror a few prejudices, and that is all they need to do.

To remain cheerful, however, one need only remember that criticism as an art is always a late development, which truth is too general to grieve over. Winslow Homer can be a powerful artist on the solitary coast of Maine, Miss Wilkins can make pictures in forlorn New England towns, but a general excellence in criticism, much more than in any other art, is dependent on the formation of groups of intelligent people, which is dependent on social stratification. Criticism, which is immediately the voice of culture, will appear only when part of the general intelligence now unsifted in our raw mass of democracy is freed and crystallized in smaller classes independent of everything save their own tastes. It is, indeed, not impossible that when these necessary divisions are made, the culture which will result will be broader on account of the influence of democracy, which must still be felt; because that influence, destructive now, may then tend to give a deeper human tone, to give to the ordinary critic, the mere spokesman of his environment, something of that wide interest tempered with humor, that free play with his material, the average mind, which has usually been the exclusive possession of the great critic of life, the Rabelais, Cervantes, or Molière. Much as we need instruction and technical understanding, requisites to any advance, we shall of course be lucky if our culture, when it comes, is slower to run the ordinary historical course into formulism, and one may at least hope that the narrowness of the barrier which will separate our future cultivated class from the masses behind it, will keep it on the move and prevent hardening into forms. Just now, however, it is natural to think less of possible safeguards for our prospective civilization than of the changes needed to begin the refining process. Therefore, any growth of social distinctions, of a leisure class, of respect for tradition and authority, is an encouraging sign, the danger of the sequence of bookishness, rigidity, and deviation from the constants of human nature being too remote to think of yet. In the mean time there is more immediate promise in the criticism of art than there is in that of literature, probably because the public, recognizing the technical difficulties of painting and sculpture, sees more often the need of training for the critic of pictures and statues than it sees the need of training and natural fitness in a man who does merely what almost any reading American feels capable of doing.

II

KENYON COX once wrote:—

> "Nothing could show more curiously than does this book the advantages and disadvantages of artistic criticism of art; nothing could exhibit more completely the qualities and defects of the artist turned critic. The introduction opens with the statement that 'only the writing on art by one who has technical knowledge of it is of practical value,' and, scattered through the pages, there are many contemptuous flings at 'a certain class of writers on art' whose 'ignorance of the technique of any art is only equalled by their ability to write on it.' No doubt the sneer is often justified, yet of many of the artists who make it, it would hardly be too much to say that 'their knowledge of their subject is only equalled by their inability to write clearly of it.'"

The combination of a knowledge of their subject with talent for expression exists in two of the many painters who write, and the qualities which they have shown tell what is best in criticism in the United States and what is needed by most of their fellow critics. John La Farge stands at the head of those painters who are American both by birth and residence, and his "Considerations on Painting" and "Letters from Japan" give the most typical artist criticism in the country, that is, criticism most typical of the devoted artist, for he has never sacrificed an hour to perfunctory writing or painting.

Looking down the list of painters who have left their thoughts in prose, from Fromentin and Delacroix and Millet at the top, through Vasari and Reynolds and Couture and Hunt, to Breton and Whistler, nearer the bottom, one finds always a keen interest in general principles, very differently expressed, to be sure, poetically by Millet, ridiculously by Whistler, sentimentally by Breton, clumsily by Couture, but in one way or another always emphasized, except in the very rare cases, where the author cared for execution only. The average artist is interested in life and likes to generalize about it, so that the talk of the studio, apart from the class room, is general, human, and untechnical. "Sincerity" will be heard many times where "values" is spoken once. Mr. La Farge is typical also of the modern painter, in being a man of experience outside of art. He has done many things, — studied law, travelled, gone into society, read largely in philosophy, science, and literature, painted, and been an inventor in stained glass. Although some of his psychological explanations border on pedantry, most of his culture is digested, and the experience of the man of the world makes stronger what the artist says.

His most general virtue is appreciation. He is never bored or even sleepy. There is always a mass of meaning in the world for him, an interest rather in the subject-matter of art than in its processes, for he has escaped entirely the fads of his day, and knows how much like other men the strongly original man must be. As Couture says of painting: "Still later, in Poussin, it reaches maturity; it has become grave and reserved; it returns to the past, gathers everything together, and gives a beautiful lesson." Similar praise is deserved by the writings of Mr. La Farge. Respect for the permanent good, gravity, reserve, the love of a beautiful lesson, are in him, and he follows his own advice: —

"First, therefore, see that your methods are respectful. Never make light of difficulties or slip easily over what you find to be obstacles. Better be gawky than flippant in your work. Imitate in your methods the methods of religious life, even if they oblige you to the lengthiest preparations. And if a passionate impulse carries you away, your expression will still have the accent that comes of previous respectful meditation."

His appreciation, sure and full as it is, and attractive as it makes what he says of other men, sometimes destroys the unity of his own entirely uncreative criticism, as where the great figure which passes through one of his books, present always, although sometimes in the background, overshadows the author himself. It was like Mr. La Farge, however, to pick out for a guide the most admirable of art critics, the sanest, the most penetrating, the one who by his depth and certainty of thought and splendor of expression can stir up the emotions while appealing directly to the reason. La Farge is above artistic trivialities of every kind, caring only for the good, wise in his judgment, showing his standards as inevitably by what he quotes as by what he says. Just as Fromentin stands out as his instructor in criticism, the great personalities are his landmarks in painting, men like Ruysdael, of whom he says that "his grave and solemn mind gives to the simplest and most common place of landscapes a look of sad importance," men like Rembrandt, Millet, and Michelangelo. He resembles his master from afar, like him filled with enthusiasm for large personalities and the noble style in art, disdainful of triviality and all digression, of tricks of execution, of any technical accomplishment that is not part of its subject, full of restrained poetry. So elevated are these virtues in themselves that one can read the lesser writer after the greater, and think rather of the distinction which imagination gives even to modest literary powers than of the differences which make "Maîtres d'Autrefois" great and "Considerations on Painting" only admirable.

Like Ruysdael's, La Farge's mind, although not sad, is grave and solemn enough to give to the common truths the importance which they alone can have. The name of death is frequent in his pages, and humility, the knowledge of limitation, the melancholy of mature happiness, are always present: "With the fatigue and repetition of the innumerable beauties of gold and color and carving and bronze, the sense of an exquisite art brings the indefinable sadness that belongs to it, a feeling of humility and of the nothingness of man." The reader of artists' books and letters will feel how typical this is of the creative painter, who loves to moralize, and who does it often better than the literary man. Sometimes Mr. La Farge's moralizings get away from him; but usually, with all their openness, they have a reserve and grace that put them high for literary art. To show how naturally they weave themselves into the subject, and at the same time to show the best of the author's style, take this passage from the letters from Japan:—

> "And I listened, until the blaze of the sun passed under the green film of the trees, to the fluting of the priests in the sanctuary on the hill. It was like a hymn to nature. The noise of the locusts had stopped for a time; and this floating wail, rising and falling in unknown and incomprehensible modulations, seemed to belong to the forest as completely as their cry. The shrill and liquid song brought back the indefinite melancholy that one has felt with the distant sound of children's voices, singing of Sunday in drowsy rhythms. But these sounds belonged to the place, to its own peculiar genius — of a lonely beauty, associated with an indefinite past, little understood; with death, and primeval nature, and final rest."

"Why," asked a young sculptor the other day, "do painters write so well?" Genuine, serious, unpedantic thinking about important things removed from the accidents of daily civil life seems to be more common among workers in the plastic arts than among any other class, and it shows when they take up the pen. Their lives are devoted to ideas, which, unlike the literary men, they do not have to beat out thin for a living. Then, too, the long apprenticeship teaches them how much sacrifice any good work demands, and often as fun is heard in the studios flippancy is rare. It is experience as well as imagination and culture that makes Mr. La Farge write so well. Never stirring, never emotional, his reflective calmness seems to be laden with knowledge of life. It is in the style itself: —

> "Far away the sounds of pilgrims' clogs echoed from the steps of distant temples; we heard the running of many waters. Above us a few crows, frequenters of temples, spotted the light for a moment, and their cries faded with them through the branches. A great, heavy, ugly caterpillar crept along the mossy edge of the balustrade, like the fresh incarnation of a soul which had to begin it all anew."

Even when no moral truth is touched, the same impression comes sometimes from the unobtrusive music of the words, as in "a pleasantly managed balance of the full and empty spaces," or "whose worn surfaces contained marvels of passionate delicacy and care framed in noble lives."

Although Mr. La Farge is always grave there are touches of light, which have their charm partly in the sobriety of their setting. There is also frequently a French freshness and pointedness of epithet that would be wit or epigram if it were not so restrained, as in the last of the modern painting tricks spoken of in this praise of the Japanese:—

> "Not knowing the science and art of perspective drawing, nor the power of representing shadows according to rule, nor having the habit of ruling lines with a ruler to give interest, nor of throwing little witty accents of dark to fill up blanks, they were perhaps the more obliged to concentrate their powers upon the end of the work; and their real motive was the work itself."

At the end of all this praise a reservation must be made; not the obvious one that Mr. La Farge is not constructive in criticism, that his wholes are not as good as some of his bits, but the more fundamental one that the style leaves the reader troubled, questioning its sincerity. The personality in it seems dual, its virtues appear to be part of the artist rather than of the man. The conscious mixture of frankness and reserve, the appreciation of every high work or impulse, the imaginative morality, the gravity, the harmony, the humility, seem to be there because they are the best things. They seem to be chosen. I cannot select passages to prove that, for it is an impression instilled insidiously by the whole; but perhaps it is most definite when the author talks about himself. A warm admirer of La Farge, the artist once spoke of him as surpassingly clever. That word seemed to give the key to my impression. The person has not gone into the style. It is not born; it is made. The man seems to be separated from the artist who selects the thoughts and phrases, choosing excellently. Pose it is not, yet it is a lack of innocence. It is sincere æsthetically and intellectually, rather than sincere with the force of an included character, and it is for this reason perhaps as much as because of the difference in perception and language that La Farge's fine passages, exceptionally just and beautiful as they are, have little of that rush of all-round living truth which in the words of a Fromentin may touch the heart of the most critical reader.

III

Kenyon Cox is in most ways the opposite of Mr. La Farge. His writing, mostly anonymous and little known to the public, is felt by artists on account of the technical knowledge, clear and severe style, and fearless speech; but it is not only the victims of his rigor who do not wholly approve of his manner. An artist who received only high praise from him, spoke with coolness of his lawyer-like virtues. Some competent observers would have criticism more sympathetic. It may well be answered that what Americans suffer most from is the leniency of their few authoritative critics. Not only do the newspaper reviewers praise under the guidance of the counting-room, but commentators of more eminence deal in the amenities to which they are tempted by personal acquaintance with the producers of literature; and even of the few who do not lack courage, the greater part think that arts in their infant state should be treated with gentleness. Mr. Cox spoke of his companions in art with the unsoftened honesty which most intelligent critics confine in public to the dead, and apply only in private to the living.

The past tense comes naturally, to express Mr. Cox's position, although he is still painting and writing in New York. It seems apt, because he has ceased to write much about the current picture exhibitions, the significant reason for this being, it is generally believed, that he found his radical experiment in frankness too uncomfortable and preferred silence to compliance. To the student, at least, there is a loss, and if competent and fearless criticism is favorable alike for advance in art and in public taste, no critic was more needed. It must be said, however, that not all intelligent people took the same view of Mr. Cox's withdrawal. "Of course," said an admirer of him,—

"Strictly just criticism is what is wanted where art is established, as in Europe. But in this country, to say practically, 'A dozen of you are trying for the right thing, but only two of you have the natural gifts to reach it,' is the kind of frankness that blights. All who are trying for what is right should be encouraged and only false ideas treated severe."

This question is obviously too large for dogmatism.

To show the suggestiveness, concreteness, and bluntness of Mr. Cox's remarks on technical execution would take too many quotations. In praising or blaming conception, color, drawing, or any other element, he never has vague conclusions, but always definite ideas, well summed up in words and full of detail. The free tone in which he speaks of even his most prominent contemporaries is shown in this remark: "Mr. Sargent is of all living painters perhaps the most consummate *virtuoso*. It is vain to look to him for thought, profundity, harmonies of tone or line; but Paginini was none the less great because he was not Beethoven, and Sargent is the Paginini of painting." Of Abbott Thayer he speaks in a characteristic way, combining appreciation of his good qualities with a frank statement of his defects:—

> "Here the manner is rough, heavy, and labored, and the color brown and lifeless, but the root of the matter is in it. One learns to look through the mannered and somewhat unpleasant technique, and one is rewarded by finding a depth and purity of sentiment which is delightful. One feels the charm of the wistful, childish faces, and one forgives everything else."

To suggest his power of stating clearly a technical principle, one quotation must be relied upon. Mr. Van Dyck had spoken of blue as a luminous color, as shown in Monet's landscapes. Mr. Cox says: —

"It is precisely the least luminous of all colors, and that is why it is, as Mr. Van Dyck says, the 'most unmanageable,' and why Reynolds formulated his rule, which Gainsborough defied, that it should be reserved for the shadows and never appear in the principal light of a picture. Blue is essentially a shadow, and that very fact, rightly understood, is the key to impressionists' use of it; for as never so little blue will at once produce the effect of shadow, one is enabled to paint on a much higher key with blue shadows than without. Instead of a difference in the degrees of remove from white, the impressionist merely gives a difference of tint, and so gets his whole canvas into the upper register and makes it the dazzling thing we know, while his pale blues, in spite of their paleness, still look like, and are, shadows. It is in the shadow alone that Ver Meer or the modern impressionists use their blue; light they invariably render as warm in tone, yellow, or even pink, either of these colors being really 'more luminous than white,' which partakes of the cold nature of blue. It is the non-luminous nature of blue that makes a blue sky so hard to paint, and every decorator knows how blue kills the light of a room. It is only by breaking blue with all sorts of warmer tones, as Gainsborough did, that it can be made to express light at all."

Even one who thinks this the kind of work which America needs should of course mark its limits. Honesty is not the only quality which keeps Mr. Cox from pleasing the public. To take hold of the people, the critic must generalize highly. His concrete judgments must be so set in elementary principles, familiar to all, that they will seem but the text for the expounding of these fundamental ideas. This does not of necessity point to Ruskinism, although a large element of moralizing and obvious poetizing might be recommended in a recipe for criticism of which the appeal should be universal. Criticism may be humanized without being moralized. If Fromentin's perceptions were not given unity by strong feeling, by a distinct point of view, by the individuality, the personal element in his style, he would not with all his knowledge of painting and writing be the first of art critics. If Diderot had not connected pictures and statues with the other interests of life, he could not have led the intelligence of France to art as he did in the Eighteenth Century. Emotional sympathy, controlled but expressed, is needed to give the critic the ear of the world — moral imagination, ardor. The human tone is what Mr. Cox lacks. His style, strong, clear, free of moralizing and of guesswork, is not alive, but formal, merely intellectual. He certainly sees fundamental moral, mental, emotional elements in the artists with whom he deals, and handles them as fairly as he does technical methods, but that does not give similar qualities to his own presentation. Accuracy, simplicity, value to the student, are in this estimate of Turner no more clearly than is the lack of the more universal elements which make literature.

"Turner's city is like one seen in a troubled dream, — luridly magnificent, but rankly impossible in every line. Repose is carefully eliminated, and mass is everywhere subdivided into an endless mass of confusing and benumbing details; church spires are lifted to a Babel-like elevation; the bridge across the river becomes Cyclopean in its stride; everything is colossal, yet wavering and uncertain, like a city in the clouds at sunset — and, like such a city, one expects to see it dissolve and transform itself before one's eyes.

"That this is a work of strong imagination no one can deny; but whether or not it is that of a great or healthy imagination is a different question. To us the imagination of Turner seems an eminently morbid and — let us risk the word — theatrical one. His conception of art was scenic and spectacular; his mind was operatic. Many of his little vignettes seem like sketches for the scenery of a *feerie*, and he would have been the greatest scene-painter that ever lived. His natural endowment was great, his knowledge of nature profound; but his carelessness of truth was supreme, and his influence, wherever exercised, has been almost unmixedly for evil."

This summary, strong as it is, approaches a danger often connected with the power of vigorous writing, — the heightening of contrasts, the omission of reservations, in order to be striking. The student does not care. He is looking less for a judgment that is absolutely judicial than for inside light on art, and he gets more from the expert whose conclusion is wrong than from the ignorant person who is right; however irrelevant the standards of the expert may be to the picture he is judging. Mr. Cox says of the Assumption: "It is clumsy, and posed in its arrangement, the figures are common in type and (several of them) badly drawn, the color is bright with the brightness of stained glass, thin and lacking in quality. . . . The 'Presentation' is flat and hard and commonplace, and the others are grimy and brown and woolly, and commonplace too." That may be true, but it may well be said that Titian is not adequately accounted for. Mr. Cox is frankly a student neither of the public nor of the past. "The earlier men, the Vivarini and the rest, and even Gentile Bellini and the much lauded Carpaccio, may, by all but the historical student of art, be entirely neglected." His judgment does not change with the time or the artist. He is always Kenyon Cox, a New York painter of to-day, clear-headed, sturdy, educated, applying the standards of contemporary execution to all time and every place. In praise it is the same. Of Pallas and Mars he says:—

> "The fulness and glow of color is Titian at his best, but Titian with a difference — Titian inclining to the blue and green of the scale and away from the red and yellow. The richness of light and shade, the glow of the lovely knees and rounded arms, and the transparent depths of shadow, are like Correggio, but a Correggio of more daring invention, and shorn of the affectations and prettinesses adored of school girls. The lithe suppleness of full muscled form, the adorable distinction of the delicately poised heads, with their shining braids of golden-brown hair, the firm hands, with their square-ended fingers — these are Tintoretto and none other; one of the first painters of all time when he took the time to be so."

Inspiriting as this is, it does not touch what makes Tintoretto part of the world's history. To appreciate Mr. Cox is to see what a narrow ground he stands upon, at the same time that one sees how few occupy it; and after all the limitations are drawn, he remains a bracing and regulating critic. He respects success in the solution of a given problem, and knows it when he sees it; and therefore he is as much needed now as others who have what he lacks, — the love of beauty and of poetry.

IV

In any criticism an interesting element is the personality of the critic, and in no contemporary American criticism is there a fuller character than there is in the style and substance of Mrs. Van Rensselaer's writing. The quality, therefore, which her style has in a pre-eminent degree, is the sense of life and some of the best personal elements. Her constant improvement in technical skill shows devotion to the demands of words and phrases; but, after all, her work remains of the kind which leaves the reader with a respect for literature, but a realization of its littleness in comparison to its subject. To give the elements of her own power, it may be enough to quote her praise of another: —

"I knew of no more delightful place than his studio, where one forgot the art, almost, in one's interest in the man — or felt it to be merely a part, a fragment, an incomplete revelation, of a most attractive personality, a most intelligent mind, a most warm and honest heart. He loved his art as few men love it even among artists; and he seemed to love humanity as do few of us, I fear, in any walk of life. A talk with him was one of the best spurs to effort, to energy, to enthusiasm of a clear-sighted and not a maudlin kind, that an artist or a critic could receive. No one could be careless or apathetic, unreasoning or hypercritical, in George Fuller's Company — no one could forget the pleasure and responsibility of his work whether that work were painting or mere commentary."

How many critics can be so serious without loss? In how many is earnest feeling at once strength and fineness? Although much that can be learned shows in this style, its worth is the way of seeing the world, the something that gives importance to elementary things said simply. The words tell us that the writer has felt keenly, and seen with an intelligence which is kind. We know that frivolous things are not part of her, that even her humor is dignified. One kind of earnestness is the most depressing fault, one rare kind the highest faculty. Mrs. Van Rensselaer, who writes for the general public, sometimes mars her pages by the direct teaching style, but this roughness of form almost disappears in the general tone of gravity and experience, of enthusiasm controlled by a sense of what cannot be said.

Simplicity is the natural expression of such a nature. Her words are common ones, not infrequently repeated. There is little ornament, no over subtle idea. Many of her pages are admirably written technically, as well as essentially, but the finish is seldom obtrusive: —

"I have, indeed, seen one or two Japanese pictures where a weeping willow looked very well. There it overhung a cascade; and it looked well because the falling lines of water harmonized with its own lines — because, so to say, the cascade excused its abnormal shape. If you have a little cascade, then, plant a little weeping willow; or if you have a big waterfall, encourage a weeping willow to grow big beside it; but do not allow one to shed its tears in the centre of your lawn, or to mingle its weak pendulousness with the sturdier, more normal forms of the trees in your foreground group or your forest-like plantation. It can never form an assent, like a Lombardy poplar; it can only form a contrast and, almost invariably, an inharmonious one. It is out of all relation with soft round-headed trees, and still more with angularly spreading or aspiring trees."

As unaffected as this and yet as far from artless, the style seems born no less of experience than of character. Frankness, expansion, amiability are in it, but above them are discretion, practical wisdom, and taste, the weight of experience of many sides of life. It seems to me of minor importance that Mrs. Van Rensselaer writes mainly about art. Whatever might have been her subject, the attraction would have been the same. One who reads her essay on "People in New York," or her story called "One Man Who was Happy," will see this attraction at its best. Her knowledge of life, from fashion to the slums, her interest in all its forms, is not so much the cause as the result of the quality which makes her charm. Active political work and historical research simply fit into the same virtue, sane but earnest intelligence applied to those subjects which are most important to the race. Literature that does not seem like an overflow of life may be charming, but it is not impressive. An instinctive sense of the reality of the world, a point of view near the centre, is needed to allow the individual to borrow some of the world's momentum. "Henry James," said a clever man to me, "has hopelessly handicapped himself by taking for the centre of his world the country house, which is not the centre of the universe." Mrs. Van Rensselaer's feeling for life, for the mass of men as the world on which classes, intellectual as well as social, are but hills and valleys, has given her some of her faults as an artist, notably some needless explanation, but that, with the other defects of form with which she started, has rapidly decreased with work; so that in the writing of the last two years the form is a comparatively adequate channel for the nobility of thought and feeling. The words every year carry more and more uninterruptedly the breadth, the warmth, the understanding of fundamentals, the kindness that make her essays and her stories live. With all this seriousness there goes the loyalty to art which makes her, as she says in her article on Stevenson, rewrite not less than thirty times to make a passage satisfactory to her in sound as well as in sense. Some faults there will always be, but they have little to do with the rare combination of sincerity and delicacy of feeling, earnestness and constancy of effort, clearness and lack of digression in thought, which combine into a vital style. To quote again her words of another: —

"A philosopher very wise in that most precious kind of lore which gives the soul modesty and poise, cheerfulness, humor, and courage; a student of human nature, not with classification and categories to fill out, but with a special welcoming niche prepared for the reception of each new human soul; a 'detached intelligence,' but a heart intimately attached to every palpitant fibre in the web of existence, which loved to love, and chose for its hatred only fundamentally hateful and harmful things like hypocrisy, vanity, intolerance, and cowardice in the face of life."

After the death of the same man, Stevenson, she wrote: "In our little world of art, in our strenuous little world of oft-defrauded but perennial aspiration, I feel that there will never again be quite as much joy in the technical struggle." But greater always than her interest in the technical struggle is her care for people, "the motley pageant of the streets," as she says, the life outside as well as in. " . . . to see the rich of New

York in all their gorgeousness one must visit Central Park of a pleasant afternoon. I like to do this myself, in the finest carriage owned by any of my friends, and to pretend that nothing else could suit me quite so well." Then, more seriously, comes the interest in "those who are helping to turn the wheels of the big, busy, experimenting world." To find the gravest note, read "One Man Who was Happy," on the one hand, and on the other, the end of "People in New York," both full of personal feeling; one for the individual, the other for a class.

"Do you know that the tiny gifts in money and food which pass from almost empty to quite empty hands in this town of ours must exceed in their noble aggregate the lordly sums that our rich folks give in charity? . . . You might see dreadful things in the streets of this region, more dreadful things in its flaming bar-rooms and dance-halls, things most dreadful and pitiful beyond words in its damp and filthy cellars, in its naked attics, which are cold past sufferance in winter, and in summer pestilential with a tropic heat. And now you might hear the desperate cry, 'Let us eat, drink, and be merry, for to-morrow we die,' and again the still more desperate moan, 'Help us to eat, drink, and be warm, just for once — for we are dying to-day.'"

To come back to the contrast again; all this is in the woman who speaks of "that natural love for pretty things which assails even the least extravagant of my sex," whose articles in a New York newspaper led the opposition to woman suffrage at the time of the agitation there, whose pen has carried weight in many political changes, who in many branches of art, although not an expert, is a scholar. The feminine quality is in every page, making more striking the picture of what one woman can do. The kindness is feminine, the seriousness, the humor, the taste, all are necessarily feminine since all are personal. It is a striking case of a character steadily conquering a mode of expression, not by the method of putting into the words only what would easily go into them, but by working at them until they received the whole personality with its exceptional richness. All this is essentially praise of her work as literature; but that work has its place as interesting criticism, because the appreciation and the power which have counted for so much in New York life, have been put in such large part into making art ideas alive to a class of readers who could only be effectively reached by a person whose point of view was widely human.

V

Among contemporary Americans Mr. Brownell is the best representative of the powers and the shortcomings of one very distinct kind of literature, which gains its strength from culture and has the weaknesses of such an origin. There are more critics fundamentally of his sort in England, and there are some with superficial resemblances to him in France, because it is from the literature of France that he has drawn largely for his education. This special study of French literature, conspicuous now in American and English critical minds, gives usually lucidity and prudence; but it instigates the attempt to assimilate qualities which seldom enter organically into superior English style, such as the studied emphasis of the epithet and the manner of intellectual sprightliness. Although, however, French models are not aids to permanent English literature, the general level of current writing is doubtless being raised by the study of them. Sentimental rhetoric and heavy truism are killed by it. Respect for attainment, for skill, for expert opinion is instilled by it. In "French Traits," Mr. Brownell's thought seems more the result of immediate observation, although there too it owes much to good books or to good company; and in "French Art," we get, not copied but chosen and reflected, some of those clear, permanent ideas which are the heritage of culture, to which, now and then, some original critic adds something; so that those who never get to the sources, to "Maîtres d'Autrefois," for instance, to Millet's letters, to a dozen other springs, to the talk of living painters, miss, if they read "French Art," much less than if they do not; for in it are given with dignity and purity the lasting conceptions, slowly accumulated, of the best general criticism; points of view merely burlesqued by many more popular English writers.

Mr. Brownell's style is studied; it verges on epigram. "To be adequate to the requirements — rarely very exacting in any case — made of one; never to show stupidity; to have a great deal of taste and an instinctive feeling for what is elegant and refined; to abhor pedantry and take gayety at once lightly and seriously; and beyond this to take no thought, is to be clever. . . ." That, I think, is a pleasing definition, with just enough lightness to fit its subject. The power of pressing a whole point of view into a few phrases without being pyrotechnic is shown in an extract, much of which might apply to the kind of literature which he himself makes.

"The neo-Greek painters are thoroughly educated. They lack the picturesque and unexpected note of their poetic brethren — they lack the moving and interpreting, the elevating and exquisite touch of these; nay, they lack the penetrating distinction that radiates even from rusticity itself when it is inspired and transfigured as it appears in such works as those of Millet and Rousseau. But their distinction is not less real for being the distinction of cultivation rather than altogether native and absolute. It is, perhaps, even more marked, more persuasive, more directly associated with the painter's aim and effect. One feels that they are familiar with the philosophy of art, its history and practice, that they are articulate and eclectic, that for being less personal and powerful their horizon is less limited, their purely intellectual range, at all events, and in many cases their æsthetic interest, wider. They have more the cultivated man's bent for experimentation, for variety. They care more scrupulously for perfection, for form. With a far inferior sense of reality and far less felicity in dealing with it, their sapient skill in dealing with the abstractions of art is more salient. To be blind to their successful handling of line and mass and movement, is to neglect a sense of refined pleasure. To lament their lack of poetry is to miss their admirable rhetoric; to regret their imperfect feeling for decorativeness is to miss their delightful decorum."

This long quotation gives a glimpse, not only of Mr. Brownell's powers, of his penetration, firm style, faultless syntax, of his clear ideas held with ease and measure, but also of his minor failures in the use of his own manner. "Sapient skill," the contrast of "decorativeness" with "delightful decorum," are each unobjectionable; but before one of his books is finished, the reader sees enough obvious alliteration to make him restless, and "sapient" is one of the words, like "suave" and "puissant," which appear with an insistence that is depressing, especially when variety might be given by better words, more ruggedly English. Other words, good in themselves, less suggestive of French reading, words which are fashionable in the vocabulary of contemporary culture, are worked too hard; among them, in their special applications to art, "composure," "reserve," "reticence," "stark," and "elegance." In judging one whose powers are shown largely in the selection of words, it is certainly not beside the mark to lay some emphasis on these little flaws of execution. Robert Louis Stevenson, perhaps the prince of those who subdue language word by word, never learned to conceal his art.

Trifling failures in this kind of skill raise the larger question of the value of this writing, the perfection of which is gained by studying the details of language. What is the style worth of Stevenson himself? It is a broad question, insoluble and interesting, the comparative worth of the style of culture, compared to the style that is a man, the style of inspiration. Does Stevenson have anywhere the blood that flows through the easy, unstudied sentences of writers whose minds were on their results, not on their tools, by whom words were used almost as unconsciously as letters? Can any self-made writer stand permanently with the spontaneous ones, with Fielding, with Swift, De Foe, or Scott? In criticism the answer is less certain; but even there the great styles, those for instance of Bacon, Dryden, Thackeray, Emerson, Lamb, seem to grow out of the idea, with an occasional pause for a word, not out of a preoccupation with phrases. The consciousness of one's language leads naturally to an attempt to overload the epithet, making what one of my friends called "adjective literature." However, this emphasis of the details of style is intelligent, instructive, fit to leaven our present crudity. It has not the unity given by a mastering thought, only a little piece of the writer goes into his phrases, a studied fragment of his conscious thought, poor by necessity in comparison to the style used unconsciously and inevitably as a man's native tongue.

Of course the attempt to judge a writer by standards so high is in itself praise, and Mr. Brownell will hardly be praised too much. "Poise," says he, "is perhaps the one essential element of criticism." It is at least an essential, and one which he has to the full. Romantic and classic art, initiation and tradition, are given equal justice by him, and even such persons as Bougereau and Cabanel have their meed of appreciation. Perhaps the thing most difficult for him to weigh objectively is crudity, but "French Traits" almost contents one who accepts with satisfaction America as it is. On the other hand, in the wide range of his three books, there is, I believe, but one infatuation, — his admiration for the sculptor Rodin. In this artist all of Mr. Brownell's comparisons must be with the giants of thought, mainly with Michelangelo; and although the superiority of the Frenchman is not stated, as Mr. Brownell never decides the relative values of contrasted styles, the exposition of the Frenchman's art, contrasted with that of Michelangelo, is so ardent that it is a solitary break in the sustained judicial tone; in that careful, comprehensive appreciation of diverse qualities which gives value to his opinions and dignity to his language. To describe his point of view more narrowly, — it is that of the literary man of intelligence; not the painter's, by any means, although touched sometimes with studio language; still less that of the man who is blind to the differences between the standpoint of the painter and those of the moralist and poet; but that of the literary man in a fairer sense, broad enough to see what the painter thinks, what the many kinds of spectators think, and personal enough to know what he thinks himself.

1896.

AMERICAN COSMOPOLITANISM

VI

AMERICAN COSMOPOLITANISM

AT a time when so many new ideas about the humanities are flooding America, it is not surprising that among our ambitious young men of the first generation of culture are many whose intellectual methods show more eagerness than measure. With no traditions behind them they do not realize how necessary are humility, repose, and care to sound ripening of the perceptions and the judgment. As their fathers struggled for academic education or for material ease, the sons make a struggle of ideas on art. They over-emphasize what they get hold of, from a deficient sense of permanent values. Though this spectacle has been seen at other times, perhaps never before was so large a mass of new ideas thrown to so hungry a public.

The men of whom I speak are more occupied with the idea of enlightenment than with the things which give light. Americans give too much importance to intellectual things, it is frequently said. Riper intelligence puts less emphasis on itself. When we first see beyond others about us we are dazzled by the idea of our own advancement. This often makes us set ourselves up as enemies of the Philistines and of all their ways. What is known to all or felt by all is unimportant. Distinction consists in seeing and believing novel things.

> "I the heir of all the ages
> In the foremost files of time."

Of the young prophets of culture whom I know, all Americans, some living in Europe, some by necessity in America, every one thinks that the only art of to-day is French or Japanese; that there has never been any art in England; that the most advanced literature of the world is the realism of the younger men in Paris; that there is much less beauty in nature than in art; that work in any unartistic employment is a waste of life; and that it is impossible for an intelligent man to be contented in America. The saying that the French would be the best cooks in Europe if they had any butcher's meat, modified by Mr. Bagehot into the aphorism that they would be the best writers of the day if they had anything to say, applies also to these critics who make such striking theories out of so little.

Of course the case can be stated more sympathetically; for instance, let us suppose a youth known in college as a man of taste comes back from some years in Italy to go into the practice of a profession. His work now is intellectual, but as far as possible from artistic; and he had cared only for artistic things. His present work requires energy, attention to practical details, and logic. Among his companions he finds none who have his instincts and his training. Beautiful surroundings, friends with leisure and taste, art, music, literature, had seemed necessities to him. To adjust himself to his conditions here and be happy does not seem possible. The cities have less art than European capitals, and repel him by their noise and lack of sensuous beauty. Perhaps he chooses to give up the pursuit of happiness, sink himself in work, and make his life a routine.

His case is not an easy one, but it may be contrasted with that of a young girl I knew who went from a small city to a great university and won a reputation as a writer, a talker, and a painter. Her friends believed that she needed only opportunity to do much in art. Paris was a paradise to her. But she never went there. She was compelled to return to her home, where there is no art and no intelligent society. At first it seemed to her a moral death. Her imagination was so vital, however, that it soon began to enjoy its own power, even in its narrow home. The girl who had dreamed of the studios of Paris, the conversation, the gayety, the freedom, the art, is happy now with nothing but what she can get from a routine home life and childlike companions. She drives about the streets and looks at the spectacle of life as it is in the little city. She takes part in the occupations of society, she delights in seeing people move and think, as she delights in watching fowls or insects. Perhaps the power to express is dying in her; she cannot tell, though she tries to keep it alive for the possible opportunity. But though the disappointment is heavy still, life itself seems the great thing to her now, so rich in its barest spots that it is worth all one's powers. Excitement, joy, fame, are gone for her, perhaps, but a deep seriousness has kept her happy. Of course, if she can, she will take the other goods,—for though less, they are additions; and she knows that now she would be in no danger of losing the essential outlines in the details.

Such a reconciled way of accepting limited opportunities seems to some who have settled permanently abroad perfunctory and provincial. It would not do to draw too radical conclusions from a score of examples; but it may be that perfect freedom of opportunity weakens as many as it develops. One man of wealth, with some taste and with no talent, bought a villa in Italy, and has never returned to America. His whole horizon seems to go no further than Italian art. If he takes a walk in the mountains, he judges the beautiful only from the point of view of its suitability to the painter. The Alps are not beautiful, because they cannot be painted. A scene is not beautiful, because the blue of the lake is in a different key from the blue of the sky. His world lies in a picture frame. Whenever he meets an interesting American, he tries to induce him to stay in Italy, where alone, he thinks, true culture can be acquired. America, he says, is in the dark ages, — a nation of Chinamen. Intellect at our universities is scholastic, dry, without life. Life for him is Italian history, talk about painting, the slang of an art-world in which he is an outsider, a hanger-on, a new-comer. The real citizens of that world, it need hardly be said, have no such narrowness. The talk, the standards, of the true artist are not obtrusively artistic. These young American prophets of expatriation (there are many of them) are in striking contrast to the thing they imitate, though they impress many who cannot understand the original. The real seer of the beautiful, who, perhaps, has painted and starved in many lands, settles almost anywhere and becomes happy. New York is full of such men. They find beauties on our ugliest streets, which the pseudo-culture of their imitators could not see in Naples or in Paris.

Among the most exaggerated of the prophets of culture by one path only are the women. Their philosophy is likely to be even further from life, for it comes often from their men friends, who parody it from the originals. I have heard a number of women, living about the cheaper places of Europe on small incomes or the lower order of hack work, solemnly preaching the doctrine that "life" is in one place and not in another. Of course it is the rule that those who have come from the narrowest environment are the fiercest converts. They furnish many rather sad pictures of the check of the deep instincts of their sex for the painful forcing of some intellectual absurdities.

We see the expression of these things in journals recently founded all over the country, which, in an average life of a few months, express the opinions and reveal the art of a few young men who think they are ahead of their times. Just now the main characteristic of this literature is that it suggests as often as it can the art of painting. It calls itself by the name of a color, — yellow, green, purple, gray. Constant use is made of the slang of art. Indeed, their only way of appearing artistic seems to be to make their writing as far as possible remind the reader of the plastic arts. Art is ostentatiously opposed to everything else, especially to scholarship, morality, and industry. The idea seems to be that art is made by talking about art, or by talking about life in terms of art. Equally noticeable is the instinct that in making one special quality conspicuous by neglecting others, they are showing originality. They do not see that in an artist great enough to give a large man the feeling of life there are too many elements for any detail to be conspicuous. The work of this artist will be life-like, commonplace, unless seen by an eye to which common life reveals its interests. Edmond de Goncourt can see nothing in "The Scandinavian Hamlet." He prefers "Père Goriot," who is newer, he thinks, and more real. Edmond de Goncourt is an admirable example of the attitude of a few men in Paris who have largely influenced some of our tawdry literature. In one of his journals he remarks sadly that in a certain conversation about abstract things, general human points of view, he failed to shine; and he asks plaintively why it is that men who "on all other subjects" find original things to say are in these generalities on a footing with the rest of the world: which means to him, flat. Readers of the eight volumes of the journal may smile at the "all other subjects," but it is at least true that on certain narrow topics of which few persons know anything, he could feel more profound than he could on subjects of universal human interest. His test of Shakspere, by the way, is an apt one. It does not condemn a man that he does not find Hamlet interesting. Many intelligent men do not. Any man, however, who infers, from his lack of appreciation, that Shakspere is not a great artist, is deficient in critical intelligence and in understanding of the value of evidence. And when a man remarks that Raphael, Beethoven, or Shakspere, was a great man in his time, but that the world has progressed, and that, as we stand on the shoulders of our predecessors, the Balzac of this century sees more than the Shakspere of two centuries earlier, we have a subject for comedy. That any critic who seriously treats with contempt any man or any institution that has a high place in the general world of ideas is shallow, an avoider and not a solver of questions which confront a man of mature culture and broad mind, is almost axiomatic. When we hear so many critics to-day expressing scorn of whole nations, — saying of England, perhaps, that she has no art, of Germany that she has only dull learning, of America that she is Philistine; when we see these critics surrounded by groups of followers, do we not wish, with some reason, that we had a Molière to-day? What a play he could make of "Les Critiques Ridicules;" or of "L'École des Æsthètes," or of "L'Américain Malgré Lui."

It would be unfair, however, to leave the impression that all Americans who dislike their country are small. It is probably true that any man who is capable of sinking deeply into life has often a strong feeling for the instincts and prejudices of his race; but it is not less true that some men of genuine intellectual passion find other things outweigh these sympathies, and live with most happiness and fullest growth in foreign lands. But men of whom this is true are usually not the ones whose feelings about America are acid. The bitter berating of any country as Philistine is usually the mark of shallowness. A New York artist not long ago was speaking of an acquaintance who had been telling how he hated America and wanted to get back to Europe. "Think of it," exclaimed the artist, who was born in Europe and loves it, "he has lived in New York thirty years, and he hates America!" That is a whole philosophy. The person who can live in a great city so long and not find beauty and meaning is a small person. A strong man may say that he would prefer something else, but that will not keep him from feeling the fulness of life where he is.

Even to-day a good deal of blame for the failure of many of their graduates to adapt themselves readily to their occupations is put upon the universities, not by unthinking Philistines, but by men of comparative liberality. Of course the days when active men in general looked with entire distrust on college graduates are gone; but many men who think that a college education is almost essential to-day, believe its advantages are partly offset by the impetus it gives to this kind of discontent with our conditions. It is undoubtedly true that the prominence of the intelligent *dilettante* spirit often makes it harder to take up a burden in the world. But to look upon this as a serious misfortune is hardly more intelligent than the old-time suspicion of all college training. The youth who for several years had roamed unfettered, talking art and literature, studying what he liked, dreaming of distant scenes, is often for a few years after graduation an unhappy creature and a forlorn spectacle; but when he does turn from his dreams of other things to an effort to find beauty and interest in what is forced upon him, he finds more than he would have done without the experience.

Exactly the same thing is true, probably, of foreign training that is true of the influence of the colleges. The men who have seen doubt have in the end the clearest faith. Many of our young teachers, for instance, who are furnishing the hard work as well as the guidance in the educational changes being made in all of our American colleges are Harvard men who for a time after graduation wandered about the Louvre, or drank beer in

Berlin, or idled sweetly in Italy, dreading the need of returning. It is true also of some of our ablest young lawyers and journalists, and of men in other occupations, — though undoubtedly the men who get this spirit strong upon them and cannot earn a living in any of the arts are more likely to go into law, journalism, or teaching than into any other work.

Americans are accused of being superficial in education and in the conduct of life. Probably the men who will remove this reproach are not those who take instinctively to the methods and the point of view that grew out of the rapid settling of a raw country, but those who feel deeply the attraction of the slower, riper thoughts and feelings of the older countries; and among those, of course, the ones who after a time are able to use this insight on the actual material about them, — not to bring foreign culture here, like a grown plant, for it is not transplantable, but to get its seed, to use their knowledge of foreign things as one element of a new perception of their environment. Goethe's well-known statement that he never deemed any truth his until he had himself conquered it is applicable everywhere. It is well for us to take what information we can from any source; but before it will do us good we must learn to find it over again in the things which we see and work with. Our deepest knowledge of life must be our first-hand perceptions, must come from daily sights and experiences. The man who lives in New York and thinks in London or in Rome guesses at life.

The question, of course, remains, whether one can say that every artist, or every student of life, will grow best where he was planted. The young artist who wishes a mass of impressions and instructions from Europe only to come back and spend a life in trying to understand from the inside the New England people, has a truth that is vital; but is it universal? It is one thing to say, "If you must return, you get most by putting your heart and mind into your surroundings." It is another thing to say, "Though you have the opportunity to live in any place you choose, wisdom orders you to live in your native land."

Though the extreme position is taken ,instinctively by many intelligent Americans, it can hardly stand the bald statement. One may argue: "The cosmopolitan is on the outside of things everywhere; he knows a great many things that are not worth knowing; his knowledge and his instincts are not in harmony; therefore he has no fundamental insight." Another may call this provincial or mystical. He may say: "It is as absurd to make such divisions by countries as it would be by counties. The more widely one sees the world, the more deeply he understands it." Each generalization must be untrue for some. Perhaps neither in its extreme form is true for many.

The question as applied to artists often ends, in discussions among young Americans, in an issue on the case of Mr. Henry James. He is the favorite example of an American cosmopolitan. Some who like his work say that, however delicate and skilful it may be, it is not large or important, because it is remote; it deals with no instincts shared by large masses of people; it is the talk of a man who has floated about, touching various societies, sinking into none, and recording, therefore, nothing but a fringe, the minor differences of the outside, gaining none of the rich color that so subtle and so sensitive a mind would have drawn from a life of natural responsibilities and prejudices. The answer is to take issue on the facts. Mr. James, says the cosmopolitan, has a more real insight, a fairer judgment, for his lack of attachment. The other attitude is partisan;

it is made intense by its lack of perspective; it is passionate because it is narrow. The large mind, unprejudiced and serene, chooses its goods from all the world and its friends from all mankind.

Obviously it is an individual matter. Mr. James may have done his best work with the life he has led, as Emerson may have done his best by the opposite course. Mr. Whistler may be living under the most favorable circumstances as surely as is Mr. Winslow Homer. Any sweeping rule is inadequate to the facts. One can perhaps say little more than that a man working his life out fully either way will have no impulse either to scorn or to envy the other method.

Granting all this, however, granting that some individuals will do better away from home, the fact remains to move our imaginations, that when our greatest artists come they will be no exceptions to the rule which has been illustrated by the other nations of the world. Probably these artists will come the sooner for any culture that leads our young men to study deeply real life about them, — to rejoice, like the strong artist, in fresh fields. A deep enough understanding will bring literature and art out of the millions of people of all races crowded into our great cities. To be a great artist, a man must know his world so intimately that he does not express it on purpose. He does not go to work to give the character of his people or his town. He talks about the simple, universal subjects, and his environment is given inevitably, without conscious effort, in every line he writes. The style is not the man only; it is the country, the race. To this height, to the largest poetry, cosmopolitanism has never reached. The constant record of comparisons is a slight thing before the work of the national artist, steeped in the color of a race, profoundly conscious of definite social and political conditions as realities, not as spectacles. It is a good education, the cosmopolitan training and instinct, a good influence for us, a refinement, a stimulant; but most of us who cannot have it should not take the deprivation as an essential one. Moreover, and more important from the general point of view if not from that of the individual, the most interesting men are not made by cosmopolitan training. They grow in the soil.

1896.

HENRY JAMES

VII

HENRY JAMES

THE ironical attitude, according to Mr. Henry James, is the attitude of the artist; an opinion which may well be startling until one learns that the artist is one thing and the poet its opposite. With irony, in his own sense, Mr. James is impregnated. The unusual shadings given to words, the complicated and facile syntax, the broken sentences in dialogue, that suggest a shrug, the frequent French, the irrelevant parentheses, the completions that are so close to repetitions, — all these have the airiness of irresponsibility about them. Mr. James does not crash into the heart of a thought with a noun. He hovers about it, pricks it here, with delicacy, then there, so near that sometimes here and there seem like one point. The fineness of his distinctions, their abundance, and the apparent ease with which they are dropped, contribute much to our sense of the futility of the world he is describing; partly because the world is so blind to all this, partly because at first these delicate touches seem to create a world all surface, a soap-bubble, as it were, in which familiar things are refracted into shapes at once fantastic and persuasive. Imagine a young American, crude, matter-of-fact, and rather bored by his crudities and literalness, meeting for the first time this spirit. Suppose him just enough irritated at and balked by the rigid world he knows to be ready to attack it, but weaponless. "Roderick Hudson" falls into his hand. He settles back on his lounge before he has read ten lines, with the excitement of feeling that he has found the needed secret and that it is a long and full one. He has read Emerson before, and has sneered at the plastic arts. Before he has read a week he longs to see the Madonna of the Chair, because Henry James has mixed it in with his universe by some flitting adjective. He longs to see Florence and Rome, because Christina and Rowland yawned and talked and influenced and came to nothing there. His whole thought takes a background that he believed foreign to it. There is a world that laughs at the limitations and rigidity that annoyed him — that is gay, intellectual, unproselyting; that is, the attractive people are all this, and the Philistines are simply funny and unimportant. He knows now more clearly what he wants to see and be. He wants to see people whose divisions of the world are not hampering, and he wants to be an ironical and unprejudiced observer. His Emerson goes on to the shelf, marked abstract and provincial. Instead he buys photographs of Italian paintings, studies atlases, plans a trip to Europe, and reads Mérimée and Turgenieff.

For Mr. James is not all the fascinating and cultivated satirist. There are forms built of the mass of apparently surface touches that are adequate expressions of the deepest and most lasting experiences. Though the author was in each sentence of the book, we realize at the end of the thick volume that he was not all there. The detail was deliciously redolent of a certain point of view; the whole that gradually appears is deeply typical of life, with much of its mystery. To quote one of the author's stories: "He lived once more into his story and was drawn down, as by a siren's hand, to where, in the dim under-world of fiction, the great, glazed tank of art, strange, silent subjects float. He recognized his motive and surrendered to his talent."

Of course there are intelligent readers for whom Mr. James's work seems almost frivolous. Those who are literal, inelastic, limited to set classifications and distinctions, find him remote, unreal, indefinite, inconclusive. They say that by nature he is a psychologist or a critic, no novelist; that in a kind of expression where he would be forced to speak his meaning he would be valuable. What they call the meaning they want put directly and explicitly. A world which is not obviously sifted for them, which is all one lump of vague reality, the end of which is to create with any methods, be they more usually seen in the essay, the novel, or any other form, the impression corresponding to that the actual world makes on us, with its solidity, its complexity, its irrationality, — such a piece of expression is meaningless to them. And to other minds, more vital and less ingenuous, it is meaningless too. Though in its most general features the world they see is the one Mr. James paints, they do not like his details, they do not enjoy the flavor of his mind, and they therefore cannot go through the many pages to get the general plan. The author himself believes that his novels were felt by Ivan Turgenieff to be hardly food for men. The elaboration, the thousand slight touches that make the general effect, bore such men. The work seems to them embroidery. They want more directness, simplicity, force. Turgenieff has an awful fatalism of his own, but it is too simple and too strenuous to come within our definition of irony. In the slang of the day, Mr. James is too "elegant" to come near to the man whom he calls the poet, as he does Turgenieff. But to his friends reason dressed in banter is more amiable, law is lighter when it speaks in the tones of irresponsibility. One who sees his matter as clearly as his manner can hardly fail to feel that he is distinguished by range as surely as by precision, by endurance as surely as by acuteness; that his insight is as extensive as it is fine, and his art is equal to its expression. This is not to deny that the variety of persons, scenes, or situations which he handles is rather slight. It is to assert, however, that with the illustrations he does use he sets forth adequately, completely, some essential springs of the mind. Though his people and his scenes have not the profusion of contrast that life has, that some artists have, the relations are there in their proper proportions, only in a shorter scale.

A limitation in means similar to this lack of exuberance is an inability to paint vividly the physical world. One understands — feels — the surroundings, but he hardly sees them.

The most striking of his descriptions have something the air of feats. It is difficult to illustrate a negative, but here is a sentence in which the picturesque is tried for: —

"There is a certain evening that I count as virtually a first impression — the end of a wet, black Sunday, twenty years ago, about the first of March. There had been an earlier vision, but it had turned gray, like faded ink, and the occasion I speak of was a fresh beginning,"

Perhaps the following description of the first appearance of Christina Light will show how he just misses the visual: —

" A pair of extraordinary dark blue eyes, a mass of dusky hair over a low forehead, a blooming oval of perfect purity, a flexible lip just touched with disdain, the step and carriage of a tired princess, — these were the general features of his vision."

The clothing of the personages and their physique seem described with effort, and so do the landscape, the room, or whatever the setting may be. The author is not to a large degree a man for whom the visible world exists, in the sense of Gautier's famous phrase. Its interest is adjective mostly: the interest of its effect on persons first, and, second, an interest of suggestion. It is rich in analogy. Mr. James feels its importance, and he usually gives its effect adequately, but sometimes one feels that his work is weakened by rather more than is necessary of direct description of the environment; one is disappointed at the unconvincing touch. For, to the reader who is best fitted to appreciate Mr. James, this literal setting is not necessary. The atmosphere is created without it; it comes from what the personages do and say, and from the author's manner of talking about them. The environment is a great bully with some of the best literary workmen of recent times. It is a very important element of art, but it does n't need to be labelled. In the main Mr. James is free from this exaggeration. He has a rare, distinguished genius, and it is the genius of an artist, but the artist is a psychologist. The idea is what gives life to his work; the personal, the abstract idea; though this idea does not exist apart from its embodiment, and is described, necessarily, when it is most adequately described, in terms of its external expression, — it is the side of final interest. "A psychological reason is, to my imagination, an object adorably pictorial," says Mr. James; and the reverse is as true: when a pictorial object interests him, his interest is delightfully psychological.

One who feels this inseparability of form and idea in Mr. James is rather supported by the discovery that his father was a logician at once acute and picturesque, and that his brother is a studied psychologist who connects the ordinary matter of his science with the mixed stream of life with uncommon subtlety and with uncommon definiteness, seeming at once psychologist and logician, scientist and poet. One is pleased also to read that at the age of seven Mr. Henry James lay on the hearth rug and studied "Punch," and that he longed to know the life suggested by the pictures. There is nothing told us of the child's love for the lines and colors of nature. It is beauty that is a human expression that interests him; that is information about human character. There is no truancy in the mind. It sticks to the fact from the beginning. There are no fables and fairy stories for it, no fancy, no forms that are not fact; and, on the other hand, the young psychologist is an artist, and all his facts have form. Later he has said that he can imagine no object in weaving together imaginary events except the representation of life. The child's mind was as loyal to the same object.

To explain what is meant by saying that, while everything is expression, everything is also form to Mr. James, may, after one has denied him any remarkable eye for line and color, be rather difficult. Of the truth of the proposition, however, there can be little doubt. He says somewhere that the most definite thing about an emotion is its surface. The metaphor is at once baffling and convincing, as his metaphors are likely to be. The thing I wish to emphasize is that it is his perception of the shapes of the moral world that gives him his distinguished value. In this bit, for instance, there is a fair visual image, slight, however, compared to the picturesqueness one feels.

"I always left him in a state of 'intimate' excitement, with a feeling that all sorts of valuable things had been suggested to me; the condition in which a man swings his cane as he walks, leaps lightly over gutters, and then stops, for no reason at all, to look, with an air of being struck, into a shop-window where he sees nothing."

These powers and these limitations sometimes lead one to wonder why Mr. James is not more a critic and less a novelist. As a matter of fact, most of his power is in his fiction, and the greater part in his long novels. He needs time for a multitude of his light touches to give to his picture a convincing simplicity. The best short stories, plays, and essays have been made in bolder, shorter strokes. In the drama, he not only misses the living touch, but loses his own charm. His dialogue in becoming shorter becomes stiff, instead of becoming intense. Directness and simplicity of feeling are outside of Mr. James's power of representation. There is a scene in "The Tragic Muse" in which Julia takes Nick's head in her hands and kisses it. It makes the reader close his teeth, as at a false note. He feels that the airy world, so parallel to the real world, so representative of it, is shattered when such material is forced into it. The comedy of his universe is "the smile of the soul," as Beyle said of French wit, and his tragedy is the sigh of the soul. The laugh and the throb are not in his scale; and the smile of the body and the sigh of the body are not there, either. His art, a firm and rounded representation of life, is no direct presentation of it, no copy. His dialogue may improve in plausibility and flexibility, but not so much that one cannot feel that he is describing a world that his imagination never saw; that he has seen the astral bodies of people and seen them static, in certain relations, to be described by him in long paragraphs of his own delicate observations, saying comparatively little themselves — speaking only for confirmation, as it were; that this fairy world of his, containing in it the essence of the interest of life for many, will not for any be visible to the outer eye, with fleshly bodies and tangible clothes, furniture, relations of actual space.

In criticism he is less successful than in fiction, for reasons other than this inability to give the direct blow. He repeats, sometimes grossly. A number of times he says without variation that, however flat his joke, du Maurier's picture has its unfailing charm; even the language scarcely changes. It may be that part of this iteration is due to sympathy, to the desire to make the length of his comment equal his interest, a desire which, when his attitude toward his subject is very simple, is disastrous. Much could be learned by comparing this essay with Mérimée's criticism of his friends, where the critic is as brief as he is when he carves his stories. Mr. James has no power of sacrifice. Effort, effort, always effort, he says, is the secret of success for all ambitious workers in the field of art. It is a secret that sometimes leads him astray, for he neglects other conflicting secrets; he fails to rest and he fails to throw away duplicates. "You cannot," he says to the young writer, "take too many notes." Without quibbling over the metaphor, one may believe it possible to take notes too constantly and with too much strain, and certainly possible to use too many of one's notes.

Another quality, which is one of the merits of the stories, — delicacy, — becomes aggressive and turns into a defect, squeamishness, in some of the essays. "Be generous and delicate," Mr. James says to the young writer, "and then, in the vulgar phrase, go in!" That parenthetical apology for colloquialism occurs rather too often. It begins to savor of literalness. We should like to have rather more taken for granted. We feel too insistent an air of distance, of fine breeding, even of condescension. We like to see one artist strictly bounded by the delicacy of his tastes; but we wish the critic to know that it may be another artist's strength to be crude or naked. The instinct of privacy, for instance, is something upon which Mr. James's taste absolutely insists. He cannot talk long enough or severely enough about the publication by M. Edmond de Goncourt of an account of his brother's mental wreck, and of the nervous disease of both of them, or of the publication of Flaubert's letters, and he interjects his respect for privacy on all occasions. It is safe to say he does not feel imaginatively Balzac's racy and unquotable illustration of his ideal of openness. This queasiness might be parodied by the story of a man who could not believe that athletes are sincerely without any feeling of shame when they run, bare to the knee, through the city streets. The critic must not insist too solemnly on his view of etiquette, if the world is to listen to him.

The one fault of the essays still to be mentioned is comparatively trifling, and, like the others, akin to a virtue, to the originality of Mr. James's choice of words, — a virtue particularly apt in a writer whose end is exact and fine discrimination; for in words, as in objects, familiarity dulls our vision, and of two words expressing a shade with equal accuracy the rarer is the one that Mr. James always chooses. It is one of his methods of sharpening his reader's mind and keeping fresh his attention. His fault is that he narrows his vocabulary by overworking his fresh and apt words. He not only sacrifices variety of phrase; he sometimes lets a word try for an idea that a more familiar term would hit more precisely. What essay can you read through without finding "mitigated," "casual," "inveterate," and other adjectives that have driven all rivals from the field and gained themselves a factotum air? They are delicious at first, and finally flat.

Perhaps, after all, however, this last word is unfair. It may be that the weaknesses of this inclusive, subtle, contemporary spirit are rooted in its strength. If so, it would be silly to object. It may be that what looks like queasiness of taste to an outsider is a part of the elegance, and that what looks like flippancy is only the more radical manifestation of the subtlety. It is, of course, only appreciation that we seek, and if in the world of a writer whom we are studying certain details which do not please us are an organic part of that world there is no more to be said. In this case, fortunately, it is of small importance whether these particular characteristics be spots on a bright art or features of it, for they are so slight that they are scarcely visible in a general view of the work that Mr. James has done, — a work of equal value to the detached student of life and to the sympathizer with special human progress. Standing alike in the world of art and in the world of sympathy, he has been the interpreter of each to the other with equal fairness if not with equal love. The breadth of the impression of life that can be got from his books is due to this broad stand, covering two points of view as far apart as any: the standpoint of the man to whom life is a thing to be lived, with emotion and prejudice, and the standpoint of the man to whom it is a lot of lines and shades that can be combined into attractive and representative surfaces. The literal attitude is to Mr. James apparently the more pathetic, and the artistic or symbolic one the more distinguished. He himself is intimate with both, and in his novels the two natures, each in many grades, are kept face to face, and each is shown as it seems to itself and as it seems to the other. Therefore to us Anglo-Saxons he has been an education that we needed, for the artistic attitude (in the present sense of the unmoral, form-loving attitude) is particularly hard for us to see. Closely allied to this conflict is the contrast between culture and primitiveness which he has painted so carefully and so often in his groups of Americans and Europeans. To these two great pictorial ideas Mr. James has given his best work, and in doing the best he could for art has done what was most fit and timely for the needs of some of his countrymen. Giving to them their own eloquence and coherence, he helps them see with some comprehension the people to whom they are fantastic. They know whom he likes to be with, but they trust his impartiality none the less, for they feel that he does not like too strongly to be with any one. His artistic friends, his cultivated friends, he sees in their limits too, although not so clearly as he sees his Daisy Millers and his Millicent Hennings. If he patronizes Emerson and lauds Mrs. Humphry Ward we can forgive him, as we can if his essay on London has more infatuation than power. We forgive him because he has written "The Tragic Muse," "The Princess Cassimassima," and "The American;" because, although in his essays he has told what his limitations of sympathy are, he has in his novels spoken more impersonally. Whether his novels can live, whether the world will take him thinned and spread out into so many volumes, may well be doubted, for he does not justify himself page by page and word by word; and one seldom rereads him. But he has been a marked man of his time and has done a good work in it.

1894.

PRINTED AT THE UNIVERSITY PRESS
CAMBRIDGE, MASSACHUSETTS, U. S. A.
FOR HERBERT S. STONE & CO., PUB-
LISHERS, CHICAGO, AND NEW YORK